MW00633833

THE COMPLETE GUIDE TO LHASA APSO

Vanessa Richie

Publication Data

Vanessa Richie
The Complete Guide to the Lhasa Apso – First edition.
Summary: "Successfully raising a Lhasa Apso from puppy to old age"
– Provided by publisher.
ISBN: 978-1-954288-41-6
[1. Lhasa Apso – Non-Fiction] I. Title.

This book has been written with the published intent to provide accurate and author-itative information in regard to the subject matter included. While every reasonable precaution has been taken in preparation of this book the author and publisher expressly disclaim responsibility for any errors, omissions, or adverse effects arising from the use or application of the information contained inside. The techniques and suggestions are to be used at the reader's discretion and are not to be considered a substitute for professional veterinary care. If you suspect a medical problem with your dog, consult your veterinarian.

Design by Sorin Rădulescu
First hardcover edition, 2021

TABLE OF CONTENTS

PART 2
Adopting and the Early Days with Your Lhasa Apso . .

CHAPTER 12

CHAPTER 13

PART 4

INTRODUCTION

Considered one of the oldest living breeds today, Lhasa Apsos were instrumental to the lives of the monks in Tibetan monasteries long before they were introduced to the rest of the world. Looking at them now, it is hard to imagine that the adorable little dog has a long history as a watchdog. Their small size means that they can fit comfortably in any home, from apartments and tiny homes to large family houses and farms.

Despite being watchdogs, Lhasa Apsos are friendly and loving, and at times, they can be incredibly comical. This is a breed that loves to be with their family and enjoys playing with people who are a part of their regular lives. It is a completely different attitude compared to the way they look. At just a foot in height to the shoulders, with long, flowing hair, they hold themselves in a very stately manner as they move around their indoor and outdoor spaces.

They have the confidence to go with that demeanor as well. They are more likely to be haughty around strangers or downright wary, as would be expected from a dog that has such a long history protecting people in their homes. They have two completely different sides to them, but only the dog's family and friends will get to see the bouncy, fun-loving side of a Lhasa Apso. They aren't considered an aggressive breed, but they are also not friendly with people they don't know. Lhasa Apsos aren't particularly patient with young children either.

Because of their more protective nature, Lhasa Apsos require socialization as early as possible. Puppies need to know that they don't have to be overprotective. Given how smart they are, you can train them fairly easily. Since they are independent, though, Lhasa Apsos may be stubborn. The best approach to dealing with this is by using a firm, consistent approach to training. You aren't likely to see them being the most obedient dogs in a training class, but Lhasa Apsos are perfectly capable of learning how to listen and do what they are told. They just aren't driven by a desire to please people or to be the best at what they do. They also tend to remain puppyish for longer, being less focused and more playful for about the first three years. This is important to keep in mind during training as it can be frustrating, especially when you are house-training your little one. Crate training is a very good idea because the dogs won't want to mess up their area.

Like many small breeds, Lhasa Apsos have long life spans, averaging between 12 and 15 years. However, some have been known to live to be close to 20 years old, and the oldest Lhasa Apsos lived to be nearly 30. This means that you could have a very long time with your adorable little dog.

This book is divided into four sections:

- **PART 1** - Getting to Know the Lhasa Apso – The chapters in this section provide basic information about the breed, including a brief history, a description of their appearance, and their characteristics so you can determine if this is the right kind of dog for you and your household.

- **PART 2** – Adopting and the Early Days with Your Lhasa Apso – The chapters in this section will help you plan for your Lhasa Apso's arrival and help you map your first month with your newest family member.

- **PART 3** – Training and Activities – The chapters in this section will help you understand the challenges you will face, as well as the knowledge you need to help you be successful in your training.

- **PART 4** – Taking Care of Your Lhasa Apso - The chapters in this section detail how to take care of your Lhasa Apso's health, the hereditary ailments, and canine ailments that come with age.

PART 1

GETTING TO KNOW THE LHASA APSO

CHAPTER 1

Is the Lhasa Apso Right for You?

Lhasa Apsos are generally not considered a good breed for people who have not ever had a dog before. It is best to have some experience training dogs before bringing one of these confident, lovable dogs into your home. It can definitely be a challenge, depending on the age and history of the dog, but it can also be incredibly rewarding.

Although this isn't a breed for every home, Lhasa Apsos can be a great fit in a majority of families, especially as they can be incredibly affectionate. Just don't be fooled by that adorable size and face—they can be very clever and headstrong.

Important Considerations

One of the reasons that people love well-established breeds is that you pretty much know what you are going to get, regardless of the age of the dog. Socialization can help minimize some behaviors, but older dog breeds are largely set in their ways. Here's what you can expect from your Lhasa Apso.

> **"**
>
> *Lhasas are happiest sharing time with the people they love so it is important that those considering adopting a Lhasa make certain that they have the time to devote to a loyal little dog that will follow them everywhere. A potential new owner must also understand and appreciate the unique temperament of the breed and be prepared for the special grooming requirements of a long haired dog. Lhasas do not require a lot of outdoor exercise but a fenced yard is plus.*
>
> KATHLEEN WALCOTT
> *Floral Hill Lhasa Apsos*
>
> **"**

WHAT'S GREAT ABOUT THEM

A Small Stature Means They Fit Any Home	Since this is a small breed, you know that they will be just as comfortable in a small apartment as in a large home. They don't require much space but aren't intimidated by large spaces. This is a breed that can be comfortable nearly anywhere.
A Long History Watching the Home	With hundreds to thousands of years guarding homes, there are few breeds as keenly adept at being watchdogs as the Lhasa Apso. They may not be physically intimidating, but with their years of experience, these dogs know that intimidation isn't just about size and risk. They can raise the alarm long before a burglar sees them.
A Great Family Dog	Puppies can befriend just about anyone. You will need to be careful with younger children to make sure that they aren't too rough with your dog because a Lhasa Apso may not be willing to put up with roughhousing. However, you can take your Lhasa Apso out on family trips, and he'll be able to join you for whatever fun you have planned for the day
Need Limited Exercise	Since he requires about 30 minutes of exercise a day, you can take your Lhasa Apso on a short, slow jog. If it is raining, too cold, or too hot, it isn't too difficult to meet your dog's exercise requirements by playing a few games at home.
Properly Trained, They Are Fantastic, Well-mannered, Loyal Dogs	Apart from their appearance, Lhasa Apsos became popular because of how entertaining they can be when properly trained and socialized.
An Easy-to-Manage Coat	They have a gorgeous coat that is easy to maintain with daily brushings to keep out the tangles. Since they are small, daily brushings usually won't take long. Also, they don't shed. This is another factor that helps to really make them popular.

WHY THEY MAY NOT BE RIGHT FOR YOU	
Separation Anxiety	If you aren't home for much of the day, a Lhasa Apso may have some trouble adjusting. They aren't particularly prone to separation anxiety if they have someone else in the home, even another dog or a cat, but you should monitor your Lhasa Apso to make sure he isn't developing this
Small-Dog Syndrome	Like a lot of small dog breeds, Lhasa Apsos can act like little terrors when not properly trained and socialized. This means that they may not be willing to put up with strangers, and they will expect people to do what the dog wants, making them extremely difficult to have in the home.
Potentially Stubborn	Lhasa Apsos are intelligent, but they have to be convinced that they should listen to you. If they don't see what's in it for them, they can really dig their heels in.
Almost Certainly Vocal	Given their long history of being watchdogs, Lhasa Apsos are not shy about barking. You may find it a real chore trying to train your dog only to bark when it is needed and teaching him that not everything is a threat.
Could Be a Digger	If you have a yard, you will not be able to leave your dog outside alone. When unsupervised, Lhasa Apsos can dig holes all over your yard, largely out of boredom.
Strong Prey Drive	They are more likely to be incredibly aggressive toward small animals, especially rodents and rabbits.
Some Serious Health Concerns	This is an ancient breed, and it is surprisingly healthy. Still, the genetic issues they have can be very serious and costly.

Adult Versus Puppy

The final question to ask yourself before you settle on a breed is whether you should get an adult or a puppy. The answer varies based on the individual or family. Here are some considerations to help you determine which age dog is a better fit for your home.

Photo Courtesy
of Pam Monzon

Bringing Home an Adult Lhasa Apso

With a breed like a Lhasa Apso, you need to be careful about adopting an adult; if the dog is not properly trained, life can turn into a real struggle because of their stubbornness. That said, adults can sometimes quickly integrate into your home with very little work on your part.

If you have young children at home, you will need to watch your dog closely and make sure he has a positive reaction to kids, especially if you don't know the dog's history. You will also need to be careful about introducing a Lhasa Apso to other pets, although most Lhasa Apsos tend to warm up to other animals fairly quickly, unless the animals are smaller, as discussed earlier.

On the positive side, older dogs can give you more immediate gratification. You don't have to go through the sleepless nights that come with a new puppy. The odds are also that you aren't going to be starting from the beginning with house training.

Additionally, adult dogs are awake during the day a lot more than puppies, and while it may take your new dog a bit longer to warm up to you, you can still bond much faster with an adult.

Finally, one of the biggest benefits of acquiring an adult dog is that it will already be its full size. There is no need for guessing how big your dog will grow to be, and that makes it easier to purchase the appropriate-sized gear and supplies right from the start.

The following is a list of questions to consider when adopting an adult Lhasa Apso:

- **Can you properly dog-proof your home before the dog arrives?**

You can't simply bring a dog into your home, whether an adult or a puppy, and let him run around unchecked. To be sure he learns the rules of the house before roaming freely, you will need to have a safe, dedicated space for your new dog. (Details of how to dog-proof your home are discussed in Chapter 5.)

- **Do you have pets that will be affected by a new dog?**

Lhasa Apsos are likely to get along just fine with any dog—and probably cats—but you will still want to be very careful since you don't know the dog's history with other animals. This introduction should take place over the first couple of months. Introducing the animals in a neutral territory will show you what to expect when your Lhasa Apso and your current dog(s) are together on a permanent basis. Even if they appear to be compatible, you still need to keep them apart for a while. This will ensure your new Lhasa Apso understands that the other dogs are part of the pack and are not a threat to him.

You will need to be aware of how your other dog(s) reacts as well. Even if your current dog is very friendly, you will still want to be careful when introducing the two and allowing them to interact in your home.

- **What is the dog's health history?**

A complete health record for a rescue Lhasa Apso may not be available, but it is likely you will find a dog that has already been spayed or neutered as well as chipped. Unless you adopt a Lhasa Apso with health issues, which should be disclosed by the rescue organization (if known), rescues tend to be less costly than puppies at their first vet visit. In other words, for the first few years, your Lhasa Apso's health-care visits should not be too expensive.

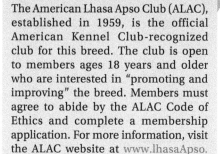

LHASA ASSOCIATIONS
The American Lhasa Apso Club (ALAC)

The American Lhasa Apso Club (ALAC), established in 1959, is the official American Kennel Club-recognized club for this breed. The club is open to members ages 18 years and older who are interested in "promoting and improving" the breed. Members must agree to abide by the ALAC Code of Ethics and complete a membership application. For more information, visit the ALAC website at www.lhasaApso.org.

Bringing Home a Lhasa Apso Puppy

Puppies are a major time investment, and a dog as intelligent and potentially stubborn as the Lhasa Apso will make some aspects of raising a puppy that much harder. How much time can you devote to a puppy's care? Will you be able to deal with an excitable puppy that has everything to learn?

A puppy will be a better fit if you can put in dedicated time for training and socializing before the dog becomes set in his ways. If you have other pets at home, a puppy is definitely a better choice than an adult because he is young and can be trained to follow your rules. (The exception would be if you find an adult that is already well-socialized.)

The following should be considered when determining whether or not a Lhasa Apso puppy is a good fit for your home:

- **How much time do you have available for training and socialization?**

All puppies are a lot of work, starting with the moment the puppy enters your care. While the Lhasa Apso's temperament is fairly predictable, how you train and socialize your puppy will affect every aspect of the dog's adult life. Training and socializing can take up a large chunk of time in the beginning, but both are absolutely essential for raising a healthy, well-mannered Lhasa Apso.

- **Are you able to show firmness and consistency when training such an adorable puppy?**

Photo Courtesy of Icey Vallesteros

From the very beginning, you have to establish yourself and your family as the ones in charge; your Lhasa Apso must understand his place in the family hierarchy. You will need to be patient and consistent with your training, no matter how frustrated you become or how cute those puppy eyes appear. All intelligent dogs have a streak of stubbornness!

- **Do you have the time, energy, and budget to puppy-proof your home?**

The preparation for your puppy's arrival begins long before he first sets foot in your house.

Photo Courtesy of Natalie Riley

Puppy-proofing your home is as time-consuming as child-proofing your home. If you do not have the time for this, then you should consider getting an adult dog instead of a puppy. (Details of how to puppy-proof your home are discussed in Chapter 6.)

You will receive records about the puppy and the puppy's parents, which will make it easier to identify any problems your Lhasa Apso might experience in the future. This makes it considerably easier to keep your puppy healthy and to spot potential issues before they become major problems.

Some people find it easier to bond with puppies than with adult dogs. A young puppy may be nervous in a new home, but most adjust quickly because they are predisposed to enjoying the company of those around them.

CHAPTER 2
Breed History of the Lhasa Apso

The adorable appearance of the Lhasa Apso makes it difficult to guess the long history of the breed. It isn't certain just how old the breed is, with some historians thinking they date back anywhere between 800 and 2,500 years. What experts on the breed agree on is the way that the breed has lived—as sentinels for Tibetan monks.

Among the World's Oldest Dog Breeds

The Lhasa Apso breed began somewhere around 800 BCE, which makes them among one of the oldest breeds. Unlike many of the older dog breeds, Lhasa Apsos were not kept to a few smaller regions. Since they were given as gifts to people in locations all across Asia, it is thought that they are related to a number of other similar breeds across the continent.

Photo Courtesy of Choo Michael Yang

It is believed that some of the more famous Chinese dogs, like the Pekingese and Shih Tzu, may actually have started with the gifting of Lhasa Apsos to prominent members of the Chinese royalty and nobility. The breeds thought to be linked to the Lhasa Apso have a similar appearance, stature, and some of the same characteristic behavioral traits.

Tibetan Origins

Tibetans have long called the breed Apso Seng Kye, which is translated as "bark lion sentinel dog." The first part of the name comes from the dog's suspected origins in Tibet's capital, Lhasa. It is less certain where the second part of the name originated. The first theory is that the name has been misspelled, and that it should be aabso, which was part of the name the Tibetans originally used. Another theory has the word being a shorter version of rapso, which is Tibetan for "goat," and it refers to the type of fur that the breed has, which is woolly, like a goat's coat.

The monks had the dogs stand watch in their temples, but they were not the only people to use these cute

DID YOU KNOW?
Best In Show

As of yet, a Lhasa Apso has never taken home the Best In Show title from the Westminster Kennel Club's annual dog show. However, in 1977, the Lhasa Apso Ch. Yojimbo Orion, owned by Elaine Spaeth, was the winner of the Non-Sporting Group, a category dating back to 1924.

Photo Courtesy
of Tracy Kiely

little dogs. Royalty kept Lhasa Apsos around palaces to act as watchdogs. Of course, they were not the first line of defense. Other breeds resided outside as guard dogs, typically Mastiffs, and the small dogs stayed inside to monitor hallways, etc.

Since there has been some question as to how old the breed is, scientists have looked at the Lhasa Apso's DNA and found that the breed has considerable similarities to wolf DNA. Over the years, Dalai Lamas made a practice of offering the dogs as gifts to Chinese nobles. This led to the breed spreading out over a much larger area, helping to create new genetic pools. It is likely this is the reason the dogs have fewer genetic health issues than a lot of other old breeds, though they do have a few very serious potential genetic problems (Chapter 17).

The breed has long been associated with Tibetan mythology, particularly with the Snow Lion. The Snow Lion is thought to be a guardian for the nation. Reincarnation is a part of Tibetan religion, and dogs are the stage before a person is reincarnated as a human. The Lhasa Apso is often the stage just before a priest (called lamas) is reborn as a person. Even Dalai Lamas go through being a Lhasa Apso, often a mythical Golden Lhasa, before being born as humans.

A Long History as a Hard Worker

The Lhasa Apso tends to be a less adequate lapdog than many other small breeds because it has a long history as a working breed. Their long, wiry, dense hair provided protection from the climate. During the colder seasons, it kept them warm while shielding their eyes when the weather was windy. Since they were at higher altitudes where the sun is stronger, their long, full coats protected Lhasa Apsos' skin from getting burned. The sturdy Lhasa Apso body has a great lung capacity, which is required at higher altitudes. The fact that they have small legs means that they are better able to retain body heat.

Those beautiful coats that offer numerous benefits of protection from the climate require some extra care to ensure the fur stays shiny and the skin healthy. Chapter 14 discusses the special nutritional needs of the breed because of the coat, and Chapter 15 provides details about grooming.

Entrance into the Western World

In 1930 or 1933 (there is some debate on the exact year that the gift was made), the Dalai Lama Thubten Gyatso gifted a pair of Lhasa Apsos to the American naturalist C. Suydam Cutting. Cutting had spent five years trying to get permission to enter the forbidden city in Lhasa, and that permission was finally granted to him. These two dogs were the first pair of Lhasa Apsos to make it to the US. Suydam Cutting and his wife were soon given a second pair by the Dalai Lama, and it was their dogs that helped to establish standards for Lhasa Apsos in the US.

Around that time, other western explorers brought Lhasa Apsos from other parts of Tibet. These dogs were brought back to Europe and other western nations, spreading the dogs around the world. They were quickly recognized by organizations like the American Kennel Club (which added the breed in 1935).

Initially, Lhasa Apsos were called Lhasa Terriers in the US, but this was corrected in 1956 when Lhasa Apsos were moved from the Terrier Group to the Non-sporting category. Not long after that, the American Lhasa Apso Club was founded to help ensure that people practiced good breeding habits to keep the dogs healthy.

CHAPTER 3

Lhasa Apso Attributes and Temperament

An adult Lhasa Apso is only about 11 inches to the dog's shoulder, weighing between 12 to 18 pounds. By all definitions, this is a small dog that you won't have to worry about outgrowing a crate or dog bed. But before noticing their size, most people see that luxurious-looking fur coat. They are a popular breed because of how cute they are, but their temperament isn't quite what most people expect. They are incredibly confident and intelligent, which tends to result in a dog that will try to take over a home if the rules are not firmly and consistently applied. Their temperament means that you won't be able to be laid back in training your Lhasa Apso.

Photo Courtesy
of Jaimie Raven

A Large Personality in a Small Body

Though they are small, Lhasa Apsos are very sturdy dogs, something that you really cannot tell from their elegant appearance. They tend to hold themselves in a way that exudes confidence, a trait that is definitely a part of their temperament. It can be harder to tell much about their body because of how thick and long the hair is, but if you opt to cut that hair much shorter, you will be able to see why they are far more physically capable than their size suggests.

Small, Sturdy Pup

The Lhasa Apso's body is actually rectangular, which is why they were mistaken for terriers for a long time. The large rib cage allows them to breathe easier, and it also means that they are more robust. The ribs taper down. Their sturdy legs are fairly short, which contributes to both their short stature and robust nature. The Lhasa Apso's tail is very distinctive as it stands up over the dog's lower back. The long hair creates a cascading appearance that looks sweet when the dog wags that tail to welcome you home.

An Adorable Face under the Fuzz

Lhasa Apsos' adorable eyes and button noses give the dogs more of a stuffed animal appearance. Many people have the hair around the eyes and ears cut shorter so that their dogs can see more easily. Their muzzle isn't particularly long, but it isn't brachial either. This means that you won't have to worry about the kinds of problems that other small dogs have, as Lhasa Apsos are not prone to the medical conditions that come with flatter faces.

HELPFUL TIP
Reverse Sneezing

Reverse sneezing is a common and relatively harmless occurrence for Lhasa Apso dogs. The first time you hear your dog reverse sneeze may be very frightening because it sounds a lot like choking or wheezing. Reverse-sneezing episodes often last no more than 15 seconds. You can help end your dog's reverse-sneezing episode by gently massaging his throat or blowing gently on his face. Just as the occasional sneeze is normal for humans, sporadic reverse-sneezing episodes can be normal for your dog. If these episodes last longer than 15 seconds or become frequent, talk to your vet about possible causes.

Photo Courtesy of Tracy Kiely

A Distinctive Coat

What most people tend to remember about the breed is the long, flowing hair. They have hair, not fur, and that means that they aren't prone to shedding, though note that this does not mean they are hypoallergenic. They just don't leave large hairballs around your home or all over your car, and the dander they do produce won't be nearly as much as a dog that is a prolific shedder.

Lhasa Apsos have hair that is coarse and straight (except for the tail) and comes in many different colors. It can change color as a dog ages. It can grow all around the dog to the point where you won't be able to see the dog's feet, creating interesting color patterns.

Overheating in All That Hair

The long hair is fairly thick, something that was necessary when the dogs lived in the Himalayas. In warmer regions around the globe, it can cause the dog to overheat. This is why it is strongly recommended to have a Lhasa Apso's hair kept shorter in warmer climates. Chapter 14 goes into detail about grooming needs.

Temperament

Lhasa Apsos are incredibly confident and intelligent. When properly trained, they have a surprisingly light, comical side that makes them great family pets. However, it will likely take a good bit of work to make sure that your Lhasa Apso behaves properly. Their strong will can cause problems because they think they know best.

A Big Dog in a Small Body

Lhasa Apsos may want to run your home, but it isn't really so that they can get everything they want. It is more likely they think that they know what everyone needs. Since they were watchdogs, they don't tend to like unfamiliar people, and without firm, consistent training, they can be aggressive and noisy. They require someone to be the leader.

Confident and Assertive

Even though a Lhasa Apso is more likely to want to know what he will get out of listening to you, as long as you are firm and consistent, you'll find your Lhasa Apso will eventually realize that you are the leader, and they will start to follow your lead. They have long been a loyal breed, and today that means being loyal to their family. This can make them wary of strangers, as they will want to put their ancestral watchdog skills to good use on your behalf.

They are accustomed to being companions. This is a dog that knows its purpose and is very good at its job. Even if your Lhasa Apso ends up having a favorite person, he isn't the kind of dog that will just stick to one person.

Photo Courtesy
of Desiree Eriksson

Intelligent and Lively

Photo Courtesy of Donya Northcutt Dallas

Intelligent dogs are prone to boredom. This means your Lhasa Apso will start looking for things to do if he's not provided with enough entertainment, and that often works against you. With the right mental stimulation, you won't have to worry as much about your dog being noisy or destructive. Training can be a great outlet, but you will have to convince your Lhasa Apso that it is fun. This is the kind of dog that knows when he does or doesn't like something, and as a result, he isn't as likely as other dogs to engage in games he doesn't enjoy. Apart from the basics (Chapter 11), you may want to find other ways of keeping your Lhasa Apso from getting bored (Chapter 13).

Warning about Small-Dog Syndrome

Given the breed's intelligence and confidence, a Lhasa Apso that isn't properly trained and socialized can be incredibly difficult, and in worst cases, it can suffer from small-dog syndrome. Small-dog syndrome means that your little dog believes that he is in charge of your home. He won't feel the need to listen to you and can bark incessantly, as well as nip and bite. It is incredibly important to ensure that your Lhasa Apso does not feel in control and knows that he needs to always listen to you.

A High Prey Drive

Even though they were not bred to chase small animals, Lhasa Apsos do tend to have a high prey drive. If you have cats, rabbits, or other smaller animals, you will want to make sure that your Lhasa Apso doesn't terrorize them. When walking outside, you will need to always be aware of your surroundings. In the early days, this will likely mean you don't want a retractable lead, as your Lhasa Apso needs to learn to listen to you instead of trying to run off to chase smaller animals.

A Great, Vocal Watchdog

Since Lhasa Apsos have a long history of being watchdogs, they have some very robust lungs, coupled with a consistent desire to communicate. Don't worry; with the right training and convincing, your Lhasa Apso can learn to tone down the barking. Chapter 12 covers different training options, including how to teach vocal dogs to be choosier in when or why they bark.

Don't Confuse Them with These Breeds

Dog breeds that have a very similar appearance to the Lhasa Apso include the following:

The Shih Tzu is the most similar breed, and it is believed that the Lhasa Apso may have been an ancestor to this ancient Chinese breed. The most obvious difference between them is that Lhasa Apsos have longer muzzles than Shih Tzu. The Shih Tzu also has a softer coat.

The Bichon Frise is a fluffy white dog that looks a lot like a Toy Poodle or a well-trimmed Lhasa Apso but is more mellow.

The Maltese, a small white dog with similar long hair, is more of a lapdog.

The Sealyham Terrier, probably the most similar-looking breed, is nearly as energetic, but the dog's eyes tend to have more hair around them, giving the breed a shaggier appearance.

A lot of smaller terriers do have a similar look to the Lhasa Apso, but they tend to have shorter hair or fur, and their snouts are usually longer. You are more likely to confuse them for a Lhasa Apso with a recent haircut – without their signature long hair, Lhasa Apsos do look like a lot of other small breeds.

PART 2

ADOPTING AND THE EARLY DAYS WITH YOUR LHASA APSO

CHAPTER 4
Finding Your Lhasa Apso

Knowing the advantages and challenges you will face, if you have reached this point, you've probably decided you can't wait to bring a Lhasa Apso into your home. It is important to take the necessary time to make that decision because they are not the stereotypical lapdog. However, if you are ready for the challenges that come with a small dog with a strong personality, you are in for a real treat.

Once you are certain you want to adopt a Lhasa Apso, you have a lot of other decisions to make, starting with deciding what age you want your new family member to be. This is definitively a breed where there is going to be a lot of work, regardless of the age of the dog, but the challenges you will face will be significantly different if you adopt a puppy compared to an adult. The age of the dog will help you know whether you want to find a breeder or if you want to start looking for a reputable rescue group.

Ways to Get a Lhasa Apso

This chapter is broken into two primary sections: rescuing a Lhasa Apso and adopting a Lhasa Apso. Typically, people rescue an adult, and they adopt a puppy.

- Dog rescues are one of the most reliable ways to get a healthy adult Lhasa Apso. The rescuers tend to go above and beyond to ensure the health of the dog.

- Shelters are usually not dedicated to any one breed. However, that doesn't mean you can't find a Lhasa Apso or a dog that has a lot of Lhasa Apso genetics and that lovable temperament.

While you can get puppies from both of these places, it is more likely that you will find a puppy at one of the following sources:

22

- Breeders are the most reliable source for purebred dogs, but you have to be careful. Puppy mills focus on producing as many dogs as possible for the lowest cost. They are far less likely to do testing and screening, so their dogs are more likely to have genetic problems.

- Pet stores may get their dogs from a puppy mill. They also aren't likely to get their dogs from a great breeder (breeders who really take care of their dogs are far more likely to be picky about who adopts their puppies).

You can find rescued puppies from puppy mills and pet stores at a dog rescue or pet shelter. You can also get a great adult dog from a breeder, especially if a breeder takes one of their dogs back from a client who did not follow the contract. Sometimes people have to surrender their dogs, and breeders often prefer to have their dogs returned so they can find another good home.

To find your perfect Lhasa Apso, make sure to check multiple avenues unless you want a puppy, in which case a breeder is probably your best bet.

Rescuing a Lhasa Apso

> **"**
>
> *I've worked in an animal shelter for 6 years. Some of the Lhasas that come into the shelter are just as sweet as some from reputable breeders. The only issue with shelter/rescue Lhasas is that we don't always have details on their past lives or how they were nurtured. And many were surrendered for having issues of some sort. My tip with a rescue Lhasa is to get as much detail on the dog from the rescue as possible and see if it's something the potential new owner can handle.*
>
> CHOO MICHAEL YANG
> *Yangchoo Lhasa Apso*
>
> **"**

As a popular breed, there are a lot of rescues set up for the Lhasa Apso. Spend time researching rescues in and around your current area. It is a bit of a time investment, but it also means you are more likely to have a better understanding of the dog's history, something that will be important in knowing the dog's health and personality. The following are several websites that can help you find a Lhasa Apso to adopt:

- Save a Rescue (**savearescue.org/breed/lhasa-apso/**) has a page dedicated to helping you find a dedicated rescue center in the US.
- Lhasa Apso, Shih Tzu, Maltese, and Small Dog Rescue (**lhasahappyhomes.org**) is located in California.
- Lone Star Shih Tzu & Lhasa Apso Rescue of Texas (**shihtzu-rescue.com**) is dedicated to finding the best homes for both breeds in and around Texas.
- Rescue Pledge (**rescuepledge.org/adopt/lhasa-apsos**) has a lot of breeds, including Lhasa Apsos.
- Lhasa Apso Rescue (**lhasaapso.rescueme.org**) provides a map of the US to help people find an available Lhasa Apso near them.

You can also contact Lhasa Apso breeders to see if they have had any of their puppies returned that are at least two years old. That way, the breeders will have a better understanding of the dog and its personality, and they will be able to answer any future questions you might have.

Keep in mind the following questions when adopting a Lhasa Apso:

- What is the reason the dog was surrendered?
- Did the dog have any health issues when he arrived?
- Do they know how the dog was treated by the previous family? What kind of training was he given? Was he mistreated? And was he socialized?
- How many homes has the dog experienced?
- What kind of veterinary care did the dog receive? Are there records that confirm this?
- Will the dog require extra medical attention based on known or suspected problems?
- Is the dog house-trained?

Photo Courtesy of Jamie Fensterstock

Photo Courtesy
of Jan-Maree Murphy

- How well does the dog react to strangers while walking in unfamiliar areas?
- Does the dog tend to be more aggressive or resource guard when eating?
- How does the dog react to children and to other dogs and pets?
- Does the dog have any known allergies?
- Does the dog have any known dietary restrictions?
- If there are problems with the dog after adoption, will the organization take him back?

Choosing a Lhasa Apso Breeder and Puppy

> *The best way to find the right Lhasa puppy for you is to help the breeder get to know you and express to them what you hope for in a pup— activity level, size, color, personality— and your home situation (how many people are in the home, children, other pets), time you'll have to spend with puppy, etc— and then let the breeder guide you to the pup they think is best for you.*
>
> KATHLEEN WALCOTT
> *Floral Hill Lhasa Apsos*

Finding a responsible breeder is the best thing you can do for your puppy because good breeders work only with healthy Lhasa Apso parents, which reduces the odds of serious health issues.

Always take the time to do your research before moving forward. Although breeders for Lhasa Apsos are largely reputable, you also might run across an individual who is more interested in making a lot of money than in caring for the dogs. The goal is to locate breeders who are willing to answer ALL of your questions patiently and thoroughly. They should show as much love for their Lhasa Apsos as they expect you to show for your new puppy; their goal should be to locate good homes for all of their animals.

It is a particularly good sign if you find a breeder who posts pictures and information about the dog's parents, documents the progress of the mother's pregnancy, and shares descriptions of all vet visits. The best breeders will also stay in contact with you and answer any questions that might arise after you take the puppy home. These are also breeders who are likely to have waiting lists. Taking an active interest in what happens to the puppies in their new homes shows that they care a great deal about each individual dog.

You also want to find a breeder who is willing to talk about problems that might develop with your Lhasa Apso. Good breeders will ensure the adopting family is capable of properly socializing and training their Lhasa Apso.

It is likely that your conversation with each breeder will last about an hour. Make sure you take careful notes during every interview. If a breeder does not have time to talk when you call and isn't willing to call you back— cross them off your list!

The following are some questions to consider when researching breeders:

- Ask if you can visit in person. The answer should always be yes, and if it isn't, you don't need to ask anything further. Thank the breeder and hang up. Even if the breeder is located in a different state, they should always allow you to visit their facility.

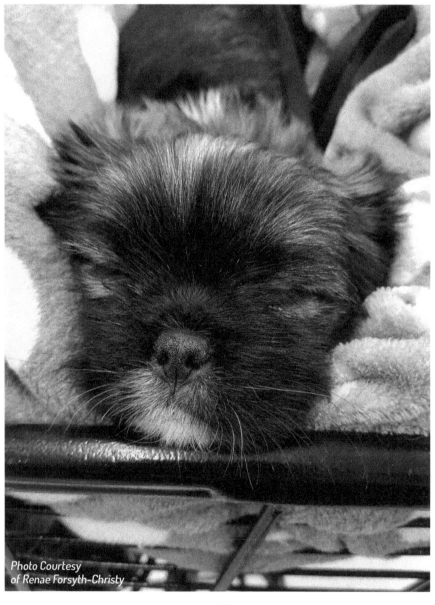

Photo Courtesy
of Renae Forsyth-Christy

- Ask about the health tests and certifications breeders have for their puppies. (These points are detailed further in the next section, so make sure to check off the available tests and certifications with every breeder.) If they don't have all of the tests and certifications, remove the breeder from your list of considerations.

- Make sure the breeder takes care of the initial health requirements, particularly shots, for each puppy— from the first few weeks of birth through the dog's early months. Vaccinations and worming typically start at around six weeks of age and should be continued every three weeks. By the time your puppy is old enough to come home with you, he should be well into the first phase of these procedures or completely finished with these important health care needs.

HELPFUL TIP
Finding a Responsible Breeder

Whether you're planning on showing your Lhasa Apso or want the predictability that can come with a purebred dog, you'll want to find a reputable breeder. The American Kennel Club (AKC) provides a list of registered breeders dedicated to performing health checks, providing socialization, and practicing ethical breeding. The AKC Puppy Finder is an excellent tool for locating Lhasa Apso puppies in your vicinity. Breeders are ranked in the search by Breeder of Distinction merit badges, from Platinum to Bronze, denoting the number of dogs they've bred that have gone on to win titles. If there aren't any Lhasa Apso litters available at the time of your search, you can sign up to be notified of new and upcoming litters. Lhasa Apsos were ranked 71st most popular out of 200 breeds registered with the AKC in 2020, so finding an AKC-registered breeder should be a breeze. Visit www.marketplace.akc.org/puppies for more information.

- Ask if the puppy is required to be spayed or neutered before reaching a certain age.

- Inquire whether or not the breeder is part of a Lhasa Apso organization or group.

- Ask about the first phases of your puppy's life, such as how the breeder will take care of the puppy prior to its going home with you. They should be able to provide a lot of details, and they should not sound irritated by your questioning. They should also explain what training your puppy will receive prior to leaving the facility. It is possible the breeder might start house-training your puppy. If so, ask about the puppy's progress so that you know where to pick up training once your Lhasa Apso reaches your home.

- Breeders should be more than happy to help guide you in doing what is best for your dog because they should want their puppies to live happy, healthy lives. You should also be able to rely on any recommendations your breeder makes about taking your puppy home, particularly about the first days with the puppy.

- Ask how many varieties of dogs the breeder manages in one year and how many sets of parent dogs they own. Mother dogs should have some downtime between pregnancies before producing another litter. Learn about breeders' standard operations to be sure they take care of the parents and treat them as valuable family members—not strictly as a way to make money.

- Ask about aggression in the puppy's parents, and find out if there are other dogs in the breeder's home. While a puppy's temperament is more malleable than an adult's, some exposure to other breeds might make it easier when integrating him into a home that already has dogs. Aggression isn't a normal problem for Lhasa Apsos, but if you have smaller animals in your home, this will be important to know.

Contracts and Guarantees

Breeder contracts and guarantees are meant to protect the puppies as much as they are meant to protect you. If a breeder has a contract, make sure you read through it completely and are willing to meet all of the requirements prior to signing. Contracts tend to be fairly easy to understand and to comply with, but you should be aware of all the facts before you agree to anything. Signing the contract indicates you are serious about committing to giving your puppy the best care possible and to meeting the minimum care requirements set forth by the breeder.

A contract may state the breeder will retain the puppy's original registration papers, although you will receive a copy of the papers, too.

If a family does not meet all requirements as stated in the contract, it is the breeder's responsibility to remove the puppy from the family. These are the dogs some breeders offer for adoption.

A guarantee states the kind of health care the puppy is to receive once it leaves the breeder's facility. This typically includes details about the dog's current health and the recommendations for the next steps in the puppy's health care. Guarantees may also provide veterinary schedules to ensure that the health care started by the breeder is continued by the new puppy parent. In the event that a major health concern surfaces, the puppy will be returned to the breeder.

The contract will also explain what is not covered by the guarantee. A guarantee tends to be quite long (sometimes longer than the contract), and you should also read it thoroughly before the signing.

Lhasa Apso contracts usually include a requirement that the dog be spayed or neutered once it reaches maturity (typically six months). The contract may also contain requirements for naming your puppy (if you would like more information about naming requirements, check out the American Kennel Club for details about contracts), details of the

Photo Courtesy of Choo Michael Yang

puppy's health, and a stipulation regarding what will happen if you can no longer take care of the animal. Information concerning the steps that will be taken if the new owner is negligent or abusive to the dog is also included in the contract.

Health Tests and Certifications

A healthy puppy requires healthy parents and a clean genetic history, which is a bit more difficult to guarantee in a Lhasa Apso due to the lengthy history of this breed. A conscientious breeder keeps extensive records for each puppy and its parents. You should review each of the parents' complete histories to understand what traits your puppy is likely to inherit. Pay attention to temperament, learning traits, attachment issues, and any other personality traits you consider important. You can request these documents be sent to you electronically, or you can pick them up when you visit the breeder in person.

It might be time-consuming to review the breeder's information for each parent, but it is always well worth the time. The more you know about the parents, the better prepared you will be for your puppy.

The Lhasa Apso is one of the few older breeds with no recommended health tests for the parents. However, as Chapter 17 details, that does not mean that you won't need to monitor your dog for potential issues.

Selecting a Puppy from a Breeder

Selecting your puppy should be done in person. However, if the breeder is willing to share videos and pictures, you can start checking out your puppy immediately after he is born!

You should consider the following steps once you are allowed to visit the puppy in person:

- Assess the group of puppies as a whole. If most or all of the puppies are aggressive or fearful, this is an indication of a problem with the litter or (more likely) the breeder. The following are considered red flags if they are displayed by a majority of the puppies:
  - Tucked tails
  - Shrinking away from people
  - Whimpering when people get close
  - Constant attacking of your hands or feet (beyond pouncing)
- Notice how each puppy plays with the other puppies in the litter. This is a great indicator of how your puppy will react to any pets you already have at home. If you see problems with the way one puppy plays, this could be a problem later.
- Notice which puppies greet you first and which puppies hang back to observe you from afar. This lets you know their personality and how likely they are to be laid back later.
- Puppies should not be over or underweight. A swollen stomach is generally a sign of worms or other health problems.
- Puppies should have straight, sturdy legs. Splayed legs can be a sign that there is something wrong.
- Examine the puppy's ears for mites, which will cause a discharge if present. The inside of the ear should be pink, not red or inflamed.
- The eyes should be clear and bright.
- Check the puppy's mouth for pink, healthy-looking gums.
- Pet the puppy to check his coat for the following:

- Be sure the coat feels thick and full. If breeders have allowed puppies' fur to get matted or dirty, it is an indication they are likely not taking proper care of the animals.

- Check for fleas and mites by running your hand from the head to the tail, then check under the tail as fleas are more likely to hide there. If mites are present, they may look like dandruff.

- Check the puppy's rump for redness and sores; try to check the puppy's last bowel movement to ensure its firmness.

Photo Courtesy of Arvi De Castro

Pick the puppy that exhibits the personality traits you want in your dog. If you want a forward, friendly, excitable dog, the first puppy to greet you may be the one you choose. If you want a dog that will think things through and let others get more attention, look for a puppy that sits back and observes before approaching you. That initial reaction should be on the puppy's terms as much as your own so that you can determine if the personality matches what you think will fit best in your home.

CHAPTER 5

Preparing Your Budget and Family for Your New Lhasa Apso

Having a small dog is good for the budget because you aren't going to need to constantly replace cages, beds, and collars. A lot less food will also be required for a small dog.

Planning the First Year's Budget

Photo Courtesy of Betty Umaly

Whether you get a puppy or an adult dog, the costs are always higher than you initially thought. You will definitely want a budget, which is a good reason to start purchasing supplies a few months in advance. As you buy the items you need, you will begin to formulate an idea of how much money you will spend each month. Many of these items are one-time purchases (or won't need to be bought too often, like a bed), but many other items, like food and treats, will have to be purchased regularly.

The following table will help you plan your budget. Keep in mind the prices are rough estimates and may be significantly different based on your location.

Item	Considerations	Estimated Costs
WHAT'S GREAT ABOUT THEM		
Crate	You may need two crates: one for the home and one for trips to the vet. If you would like, you can have just one crate; it's usually a matter of personal preference. The crate should be a comfortable space where the puppy will sleep and rest.	Wire crate: $60 to $350 Portable crate: $35 to $200
Bed	This will be placed in the crate.	$10 to $55
Leash	It should be short in the beginning because you need to be able to keep your puppy from getting overly excited and running to the end of a long line.	Short leash: $6 to $15 Retractable: $8 to $25
Doggie bags for walks	If you walk at dog parks, this won't be necessary. For those who don't have daily access to bags, it is best to purchase packs to ensure you don't run out.	Singles cost less than $1 each. Packs: $4 to $16
Collar	Make sure you check how tight the collar is as your dog grows up.	$10 to $30
Tags	These will likely be provided by your vet. At a minimum, your Lhasa Apso should have a tag with your address on it in case the pup escapes.	Contact your vet before purchasing to see if the required rabies tags include your contact info.
Puppy food	You will need to purchase specific puppy food in the beginning. Adult dog food is more expensive. The larger the bag of dog food, the higher the cost, but also the fewer times you will need to purchase food.	$9 to $90 per bag
Water and food bowls	These will need to be kept in the puppy's area. If you have other dogs, you will need separate bowls for the puppy.	$10 to $40

Item	Considerations	Estimated Costs
WHAT'S GREAT ABOUT THEM		
Toothbrush/ Toothpaste	You will need to brush your Lhasa Apso's teeth regularly, so plan to buy more than one toothbrush during the first year.	$2.50 to $14
Hairbrush	Lhasa Apso coats are easy to maintain if you brush them daily. When they are puppies, brushing offers a fantastic way to bond.	$3.50 to $20

You will need to pay attention to when items need to be replaced based on your dog's size. Ultimately, you need to establish a budget for the initial costs, then create a second budget for items that will need to be replaced. Plan to revisit this list at the end of every year so you can make sure your dog remains comfortable and happy.

When you contact a vet to plan your first visit with your Lhasa Apso, request an estimate for costs for that first year. The cost is substantially different for shots in a major city than in a rural area. Use the rough estimate for shots and other vet costs, and add it to your budget planning for that first year—as well as getting that first vet visit on your calendar.

Instructing Your Children

In order to make your puppy feel comfortable in its new home, you must make sure your children are careful and gentle with the dog, whether you adopt a puppy or an adult dog. Since Lhasa Apsos look like living stuffed animals, some kids may try to treat the puppy like a toy. Take the time to make sure your children follow all of the "puppy rules" from the very beginning to ensure your puppy feels safe, happy, and isn't accidentally injured.

The following are the Five Golden Rules your children should follow from day one. They apply both to puppies and adult Lhasa Apsos:

1. Always be gentle and respectful.
2. Do not disturb the puppy during mealtime.
3. Chase is an outside game.

4. The Lhasa Apso should always remain firmly on the ground. Never pick him up.

5. All valuables should be kept out of the puppy's reach.

Since your kids are going to ask why these rules are necessary, the following are some explanations you can use. If necessary, modify the discussion to meet the audience—what you say to a toddler is a lot different than what you should tell a teen about playing with your Lhasa Apso.

Lhasa Apsos are not particularly fond of smaller children, so it will be essential to ensure that you don't leave young children alone with your new dog. They must be constantly monitored.

Always Be Gentle and Respectful

Little Lhasa Apso puppies are ridiculously cute and cuddly, but they are also more fragile than adult dogs. At no time should anyone be rough with a puppy. It is important to be respectful of your puppy to help him learn to also be respectful toward people and other animals.

Photo Courtesy of Deb Stover

This rule must be applied consistently every time your children play with your puppy. Be firm if you see your children getting too excited or rough. You don't want the puppy to get overly excited either because he might end up nipping or biting someone. If he does, it won't be his fault because he is still learning. Make sure your children understand the possible repercussions if they get too rough.

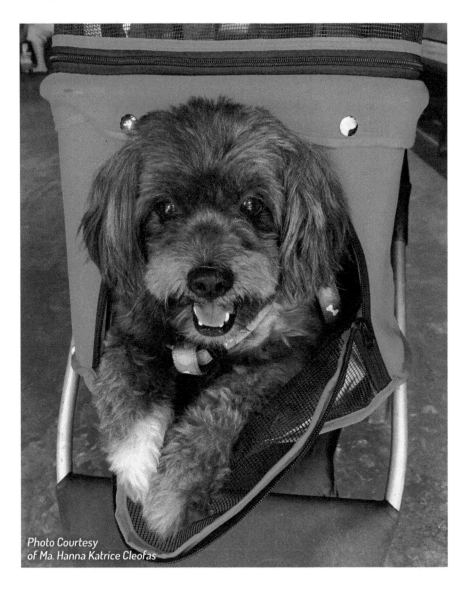

Photo Courtesy
of Ma. Hanna Katrice Cleofas

Mealtime

Lhasa Apsos can be protective of their food, especially if you rescue a dog that has previously had to fend for himself. Even if you have a puppy, you don't want him to feel insecure during his mealtime because he will learn to be aggressive whenever he eats. Save yourself, your family, and your dog's future problems by making sure mealtime is your dog's time alone. Teach your children their own mealtime is off-limits to the puppy, as well.

HELPFUL TIP
Grooming Costs

One of the costs associated with having a Lhasa Apso is grooming. While much of your dog's grooming will take place at home in the form of daily brushing, teeth cleaning, and occasional baths, your dog will also require haircuts at the groomer. Hair trimming should be done about every six weeks. Depending on your dog's activity level and your dedication to brushing, you may need to see the groomer more frequently. Price can vary from groomer to groomer, but you can expect to pay anywhere from $40 to $80 for a haircut at the groomer.

No feeding your new dog from the table! From toddlers to teens, this is something you'll really need to emphasize—particularly for foods that your kids don't like. Lhasa Apsos are pets, not garbage disposals, and no amount of cute, puppy eyes should be rewarded with scraps from the table. That is a recipe for disaster, as it will get harder to convince your dog to stop begging if other people aren't following your rules.

Chase

Make sure your children understand why a game of chase is perfect for the outdoors (though you'll need to monitor things), but inside the house, chase is off limits!

Running inside your home gives your Lhasa Apso puppy the impression your home isn't safe for him because he is being chased; it also teaches your puppy that running indoors is allowed, which can be dangerous as the dog gets older and bigger. One of the last things you want to see is your adult Lhasa Apso (even if he isn't very big) go barreling through your home—knocking into people and furniture—because he learned it was fine for him to run in the house when he was a puppy!

Paws on the Ground

It doesn't matter if your Lhasa Apso looks like a stuffed animal—he is a living, breathing creature, and he needs to have his paws on the ground. Even though you might want to carry your new family member around or play with the pup like a baby, you and your family will have to resist that urge. The younger your children are, the more difficult it will be for them to understand the difference. It is so tempting to treat the puppy like a baby by carrying him around, but this is uncomfortable and unhealthy for the puppy.

Older children will quickly learn that a puppy's nip or bite hurts a lot more than one would think. Those little teeth are quite sharp, and if a dog nips, he could accidentally be dropped—no one wants that to happen. If your children are never allowed to pick up the puppy, things will be a lot better for everyone involved. Remember, this also applies to you, so don't make things difficult by doing something you constantly tell your children not to do.

HELPFUL TIP
Building a Dog Run

If dog-proofing your entire backyard is too big of a task, consider dedicating a portion of your yard to your dog by building a fenced dog run. This area can be made accessible to the house via a doggie door or from the yard by a gate. It can be a permanent structure or a moveable one. Keep in mind that the run should be at least partially shaded during the summer, and your dog should always have access to water. Some dogs like to dig, so keep this in mind when leaving your dog unattended in the run.

Keep Valuables Out of Reach

Your kids will be less than happy if their personal possessions are chewed up by an inquisitive puppy, so teach them to put toys, clothes, and other valuables far out of the puppy's reach.

Preparing Your Current Dogs and Cats

Lhasa Apsos don't tend to be picky in the beginning. Puppies want to love everyone—people, dogs, and cats. To get the most well-rounded dog possible, though, you should start socializing him with your other dogs or pets when he is still a puppy. In most cases, this is a fairly straightforward process as long as your pets are comfortable with you bringing a puppy into their home.

The following are important tasks you should complete when preparing your current pets for the new arrival:

- Set a schedule for activities and the people who will need to participate.
- Preserve your current dog's favorite places and furniture; make sure your current dog's toys and other personal items are not in the puppy's space.
- Have playdates at your home to observe your dog(s) reactions to having an addition to the house.

Stick to a Schedule

It's essential to have a schedule. Obviously, the puppy is going to receive a lot of attention in the beginning, so you need to make a concerted effort to be sure your current pet(s) know you will still care for them. Set a specific time in your schedule when you can show your current dog(s) how much you love him, and make sure you don't stray from that schedule after the puppy arrives.

When you bring the puppy home, plan to have at least one adult present for each dog you have in your home. If you have a cat in the home, the introduction will need to be slow and methodical. If you bring home an adult Lhasa Apso, you will need to be careful and keep the dog and cat separate when you aren't around to monitor them. Over time, it is likely they will learn to be fine with each other.

Having a schedule in place for your other dogs will make it easier to follow the plan with the puppy. Once he has arrived, your puppy is going to eat, sleep, and spend most of the day and night in his assigned space. This means your puppy's space cannot block your current canine's favorite furniture, bed, or anywhere he rests during the day. None of your current dog's "stuff" should be in the puppy's area either; this includes toys. You don't want your older dog to feel as if the puppy is taking over his territory. Make sure your children also understand to never put your current dog's things in the puppy's area!

Photo Courtesy of Jade Ruddock

Your dog and your puppy will need to be kept apart at the beginning (even if they seem friendly) until your puppy has received his vaccinations. Puppies are more susceptible to illness during these early days, so wait until the puppy is protected from possible diseases before the dogs spend time together. Leaving the puppy in his puppy space will keep them separated during this critical time.

Helping Your Dog Prepare – Extra at Home Playdates

The following explains strategies that will help prepare your current pooch for the arrival of your puppy:

- Consider the personality of your dog to predict what might happen when the puppy arrives. If your current dog loves other dogs, this will probably hold true when the puppy shows up. If your current dog is territorial, you will need to be cautious when introducing the two dogs, at least until the Lhasa Apso has become part of the pack. Excitable dogs need special attention to keep from getting agitated when a new dog comes home. You don't want your current dog to be so excited that he makes the Lhasa Apso feel threatened.

- Consider the times when unfamiliar dogs have been in your home. How did your current dog react to these other furry visitors? If your canine becomes territorial, be cautious when introducing your new pup. If you have never invited another dog into your home, organize a playdate with other dogs before your Lhasa Apso puppy arrives. You need to know how your current furry babies will react to new dogs in the house so that you can properly prepare. Meeting a dog at home is quite different from encountering one outside the home.

- Think about your dog's interactions with other dogs for as long as you have known him. Has your dog shown protective or possessive behavior, either with you or others? Food is one of the reasons dogs will display aggression because they don't want anyone eating what is theirs. Some dogs can be protective of people and toys, too.

- If you know someone who owns a Lhasa Apso, organize a playdate so that your current dog becomes aware of the temperament of a Lhasa Apso.

These same rules apply, no matter how many dogs you have. Think about their individual personalities as well as how they interact together. Similar to humans, you may find when your dogs are together, they act differently. This is something you will need to keep in mind as you plan their first introduction. (Details of how to introduce your current dog(s) and your new puppy—plus how to juggle the two new personalities—are included in Chapter 9.)

CHAPTER 6
Preparing Your Home and Schedule

It doesn't matter whether you bring home a puppy or adult Lhasa Apso—the amount of preparation you will have to do before bringing the dog home is going to be roughly the same. Since the adult version doesn't get very big and the breed is intelligent, you are going to need the same kind of dog-proofing to keep your Lhasa Apso from getting into places where you don't want him to go.

Photo Courtesy of Jacqueline and Deanna Smerdel

It's almost exactly like child-proofing your home prior to the arrival of a baby or toddler. Protecting your Lhasa Apso is the priority. Even after you've completed the initial preparations, a weekly review leading up to your Lhasa Apso's arrival is necessary to make sure you don't miss anything and that everything is in place. Your new family member should have a safe space that includes all of the essentials. This will help to make your dog more comfortable and make the initial arrival a great experience for everyone.

Photo Courtesy of Renae Forsyth-Christy

Lhasa Apsos require proof that you are a leader they should follow, so you will need to earn your new family member's respect. This is why it is absolutely essential to ensure that you are firm and consistent when you are training and working with your Lhasa Apso. When they understand that you mean what you say, that will go a long way to letting them know why they should listen to you.

Creating a Safe Space for Your Dog or Puppy

> *Puppies, like children, are inquisitive about everything, so keeping them confined to a limited area when then cannot be closely supervised keeps them out of trouble. But, never put your Lhasa behind a closed door! This would be extremely frustrating to the inborn guardian nature of a Lhasa. A puppy play pen works well, or a baby gate, so they are free to observe the world beyond.*
>
> KATHLEEN WALCOTT
> *Floral Hill Lhasa Apsos*

*Photo Courtesy
of Choo Michael Yang*

Your new dog will need a dedicated space that includes a crate, food and water bowls, pee pads, and toys. All of these things should be in the area where the puppy will stay when you are not able to give him attention. The puppy's space should be gated so that your Lhasa Apso cannot get out and young children (or dogs) cannot get in. It should be a safe space where the puppy can see you going about your usual business and feel comfortable.

An adult Lhasa Apso will need a similar setup as a puppy, with all of the same items, but you can give the adult dog a bigger area. Pee pads may be necessary while the adult dog adjusts to the new environment, even if the dog is already house-trained.

Crates

Crate training (discussed in detail in Chapter 7) is much more likely to be difficult if you have a crate that is too big, too small, or too uncomfortable for your dog to feel like it is a safe place. To make training easier, be sure the crate and bedding are set up and ready before your dog arrives. A small, cozy space will help your dog feel comfortable while also dissuading him from using it as a restroom since he won't be able to get away from any mess he makes.

Never treat the crate like it is a prison for your puppy. It's meant to be a safe haven after overstimulation or when it's time to sleep. Ensure your dog never associates the crate with punishment or negative emotions. You can also get your puppy a carrying crate in the early days to make trips to the vet easier.

Puppy-Proof/Dog-Proof the House

> *Lhasa Apsos like to climb and be up high. Assume they can get to just about anything. Be very watchful the first few days and get an idea what needs to be safeguarded. Don't assume just because something is up on a table it can't be reached. We sometimes liken these dogs to goats. They will eat anything!*
>
> CARLA VARNEY
> *Hi Tide Lhasa Apsos*

The most dangerous rooms and items in your home will be as dangerous to your puppy as if he were a little baby. The biggest difference is your Lhasa Apso is going to become mobile much faster than a child. He will get into dangerous situations immediately if you don't eliminate all the hazards before his arrival. Be aware that puppies will try to eat virtually anything! Nothing is safe—not even your furniture—and they will also gnaw on wood and metal or clothing. Anything within reach is considered fair game!

Keep this in mind as you go about puppy-proofing your home. You will need to look for all of these dangers and make sure they are removed before your Lhasa Apso arrives, whether the dog is a puppy or an adult.

Plant Dangers

You will need to be mindful of the plants in and around your home that could be hazardous to your dog. The following are various plants that should not be within your dog's reach. Remember to check both inside and outside your home.

Photo Courtesy of Bianca Chad

46

Mildly Toxic	Mildly to Moderately Toxic	Moderately Toxic	Moderately to Highly Toxic	Highly Toxic
Asparagus Fern	Aloe	Alocasia	Cactus	Brunfelsia
Begonia	Amaryllis	Arrowhead	Kalanchoe	Desert Rose
Ficus Benjamina	Calla Lily	Dieffenbachia		Flame Lily
Flamingo Flower	Cyclamen	Dracaena Fragrans		Kaffir Lily
Gardenia	Dracaena	English Ivy		Oleander
Geranium	Philodendron	Eucalyptus		Sago Palm
Golden Pothos		Peyote		Bird of Paradise (Strelitzia)
Jade Plant				
Schefflera				
Ti Plant				

Indoor Hazards and Fixes

A Lhasa Apso will be an avid explorer, wanting to get into everything if given the opportunity. Get on your hands and knees to view each room from your Lhasa Apso's perspective prior to the dog's arrival.

Hazards	Fixes	Time Estimate
KITCHEN		
Poisons	Keep in secure, childproof cabinets or on high shelves.	30 min.
Trash Cans	Use a lockable trash can or keep it in a secure location.	10 min.
Appliances	Make sure all cords are out of reach.	15 min.
Human Food	Keep out of reach.	Constant (Start making it a habit!)

Hazards	Fixes	Time Estimate
FLOORS		
Slippery Surfaces	Put down rugs or special mats designed to stick to the floor.	30 min. – 1 hour
Training Area	Train your Lhasa Apso on nonslip surfaces.	Constant
BATHROOMS		
Toilet Brush	Either have one that locks into the container or keep the brush out of reach.	5 min.
Poisons	Keep in secure, childproof cabinets or on high shelves.	15–30 min.
Toilets	Keep lids closed. Do not use automatic toilet-cleaning chemicals.	Constant (Start making it a habit!)
Cabinets	Keep locked with childproof locks.	15–30 min.
LAUNDRY ROOM		
Clothing	Store clean and dirty clothes off the floor and out of reach.	15–30 min.
Poisons (bleach, pods/detergent, dryer sheets, and misc. poisons)	Keep in secure, childproof cabinets or on high shelves.	15 min.
AROUND THE HOME		
Plants	Keep off the floor.	45 min. – 1 hour
Trash Cans	Have a lockable trash can or keep it in a secure location.	10–30 min.
Electrical Cords/Window Blind Cords	Hide cords or make sure they are out of reach; pay particular attention to entertainment and computer areas.	1–1.5 hours
Poisons	Check to make sure there aren't any in reach (WD40, window/screen cleaner, carpet cleaner, air fresheners); move all poisons to a central, locked location.	1 hour
Windows	Be sure cords are out of reach in all rooms.	1–2 hours

Hazards	Fixes	Time Estimate
Fireplaces	Store cleaning supplies and tools where the puppy can't get into them. Cover the fireplace opening with something the puppy can't knock over.	10 min.
Stairs	Cordon off so that your puppy can't go up or down the stairs; make sure to test all puppy gates for safety.	10–15 min.
Coffee Tables/ End Tables/ Nightstands	Clear of dangerous objects (e.g., scissors, sewing equipment, pens, and pencils) and all valuables.	30–45 min.

If you have a cat, keep the litter box off the floor. It needs to be somewhere that your cat can easily get to it, but your Lhasa Apso cannot. Since this involves training your cat, it's something you should do well in advance of the dog's arrival. You don't want your cat to undergo too many significant changes all at once. The new canine in the house will be enough of a disruption! If your cat associates the change with your Lhasa Apso, you may find the feline refusing to use the litter box.

To get the litter box out of your dog's reach, you'll need to put it up high and preferably somewhere that doesn't have a chair that your dog can use. Clever pups can figure out how to get to places where you think they wouldn't be able to go.

Finally, in case of problems, be sure your vet's number is posted on the fridge and in at least one other room in the house. Even if the number is programmed into your phone, family members or dog sitters will still need to know who to call.

Outdoor Hazards and Fixes

The area outside your home also needs dog-proofing. As with the inside, you will need to check your outdoor preparations by getting down low and inspecting all areas from a puppy's perspective. Remember to also post the vet's number in one of the sheltered outdoor areas in case of an emergency.

Hazards	Fixes	Time Estimate
GARAGE		
Poisons	Keep in secure, childproof cabinets or on high shelves (e.g., car chemicals, cleaning supplies, paint, lawn care) – this includes fertilizer.	1 hour
Trash Bins	Keep them in a secure location.	5 min.
Tools (e.g., lawn, car, hardware, power tools)	Make sure all cords are kept out of reach and never hang over the side of surfaces.	30 min. – 1 hour
Equipment (e.g., sports, fishing)	Keep out of reach, and never allow them to hang over the side of surfaces.	Constant (Start making it a habit!)
Sharp Implements	Keep out of reach, and never allow them to hang over the side of surfaces.	30 min.
Bikes	Store off the ground or in a place the Lhasa Apso cannot get to (to keep the pup from biting the tires).	20 min.
FENCING (CAN BE DONE CONCURRENTLY)		
Breaks	Fix any breaks in the fencing. You need to make sure your Lhasa Apso can't easily get out of your yard.	30 min. – 1 hour
Gaps	Fill in any gaps so your Lhasa Apso doesn't escape.	30 min. – 1 hour
Holes/Dips at Base	Fill in any area that can be easily crawled under.	1–2 hours
YARD		
Poisons	Don't leave any poisons in the yard.	1–2 hours
Plants	Verify that low plants aren't poisonous; fence off anything that is (such as grapevines).	45 min. – 1 hour

If you have a pool, make sure it is secure so that your dog cannot get into it without your help. Covers may not always be enough (especially for intelligent breeds that may want to swim on their own terms), so make sure to have fencing or some other kind of deterrent to keep your Lhasa Apso safe. Even if your dog loves swimming, make sure you are always around

Photo Courtesy
of David A Torres

when your dog is in the pool. Lhasa Apsos can swim, but usually not for long, so make sure that your dog is protected.

Never leave your Lhasa Apso alone in the garage, even when the dog is an adult. Your puppy may be in the garage when you take car trips, which is why it is important to puppy-proof this area.

Schedule fence inspections at least once a month after bringing home your new dog. Lhasa Apsos are proficient diggers, which means you are going to need to see if your pup has managed to create holes. This is also why you can never leave your Lhasa Apso alone outside. You will always need to attend to your dog when he goes out to the bathroom or to play because when he is bored, he will very likely start to dig. You don't want to put him out to use the bathroom only to find he has escaped in the five minutes you left him outside alone.

Consider setting up a designated digging place for your Lhasa Apso. They aren't notoriously big diggers, but you never know what your dog will do when bored.

Choosing Your Veterinarian

You should choose a vet before you bring your dog home because scheduling a veterinary appointment may take a while. Fortunately, you'll probably find vets who have some experience with the breed.

Every dog, regardless of age, should see a vet within the first forty-eight hours of its arrival home. The point is to establish your dog's baseline health. This may also be a requirement included in the contract with the breeder. Twenty-four hours is strongly recommended to make sure your dog is healthy, but this may not always be possible, which is why many places say to have it done within 48 hours. If there is a vet near you who specializes in or has worked with Lhasa Apsos before, that will be best for your pup.

The following are some things to consider when looking for a vet:

- What is the vet's level of familiarity with Lhasa Apsos?
- The vet doesn't have to be a specialist, but a vet with experience with the breed is helpful.
- How far from your home is the vet?
- You don't want the vet to be more than thirty minutes away in case of an emergency.
- Is the vet available for emergencies after hours, or can they recommend a vet in case of an emergency?
- Is the vet part of a local veterinary hospital, or does the vet refer patients to a local pet hospital?
- Is the vet one of several partners, or do they work alone? If the vet belongs to a partnership, can your dog see the same vet for all office visits?
- How are appointments booked?
- Can other services be performed at the clinic, such as grooming and boarding?
- Is the vet accredited?
- What is the price for the initial visit? What are the prevailing costs for routine visits that might include such things as shots?
- What tests and checks are performed during the initial visit?
- Can you visit the vet you are considering before you bring your dog home?
- If so, inspect the office environment and ask if you can speak to the vet. The vet should be willing to put you at ease and answer your questions. Even though a vet's time is valuable, they should take a few minutes to help you feel confident about your decision to trust them with your new dog's health.

CHAPTER 7

Bringing Your Lhasa Apso Home

> *It is best to bring your new puppy home when you have a few days with extra time to get to know each other. The first couple of nights are sometimes a little rough as puppy adjusts to being without Mama and siblings. A crate at your bedside with a blanket and a puppy size plush toy to snuggle with works well as you can reach down and reassure baby puppy whenever they wake up and whimper. This is a nice way to begin your bonding process. During the day let puppy gradually become familiar with their new surroundings, their dining area and make frequent trips to the desired potty area. Baby puppies tire out and need naps so make sure puppy has a quiet, safe area for this purpose.*
>
> KATHLEEN WALCOTT
> *Floral Hill Lhasa Apsos*

When your Lhasa Apso finally arrives, it will definitely be a time of excitement and chaos. Between acclimating your dog to a new home and getting everyone on the same page (something that becomes increasingly difficult the more people and pets you have), you will definitely have your work cut out for you. Take the time to enjoy your newest family member's arrival, but also be aware of how overwhelming the experience can be for your dog.

This chapter covers how to introduce your new Lhasa Apso to your home. If you already have a dog, refer to Chapter 8 because you will need to introduce the animals outside of the home before your pup makes that grand entrance. Once you understand how to introduce dogs to each other, come back to this chapter to learn how to introduce your new family member to your home and any family members who weren't able to make the initial meet and greet.

If you don't have dogs, read ahead to see what to expect and how to make the experience more enjoyable for your Lhasa Apso.

Final Preparations and Planning

If you are bringing home a puppy, there are good odds that there will be a lot of anxiety and nervousness. Adult dogs are less likely to feel this way unless they were at their previous home long enough to get comfortable (this is usually not the case at shelters or similar rescues), but they will still feel some levels of anxiety and be wary in their new surroundings. You can try to prepare to minimize the negative emotions, starting with taking time off from work during the first twenty-four to forty-eight hours; the best-case scenario would have you at home for the first week or two. The more time you dedicate to helping your new little friend become accustomed to his surroundings, the better.

Photo Courtesy
of Alyson Hunter

Ensure You Have Food and Other Supplies on Hand

The day before your Lhasa Apso arrives, review the list you created in Chapter 5 and do a quick check to ensure you have everything you need. Take a few moments to consider if there is anything you are missing. This will keep you from having to rush out for additional supplies after the arrival of your new family member.

Design a Tentative Puppy Schedule

Prepare a tentative schedule to help you get started over the course of the first week. Your days are about to get remarkably busy, so you need somewhere to begin before your puppy arrives. As you settle more into a routine, you can update that schedule, so it isn't set in stone. Consider it more of a guideline so that you don't forget important tasks, especially taking your dog out for regular restroom breaks.

The following are three key areas to establish before your puppy arrives:

- Feeding
- Training (including house-training)
- Playing

When you bring home a puppy, you may be expecting a ball of high energy. However, puppies of any breed (no matter how active they will be later) sleep between 18 and 20 hours per day. Having a predictable sleep schedule will help your puppy grow up to be healthier. Plan eating times, bathroom breaks, and playtime around your puppy's sleep schedule.

In the beginning, you won't need to worry about making sure that your puppy is tired out by the end of the day. His stamina will build fairly quickly, though; by the end of the first year, your pup will be a lot more active! As your pup starts to sleep less and play more, he will need 30 to 60 minutes of daily physical activity. In the early days, your puppy's schedule will revolve around sleeping and eating, with some walking and socialization. Waking hours will include training and play.

Lhasa Apsos age slower than a lot of other breeds, so they can act like puppies up until they are three years old. This may also mean that it takes longer for the puppy to make the shift to a more active schedule. Every puppy is different, even within a single breed, so adjust the schedule based on the changes you see with your own puppy.

Do a Quick Final Puppy-Readiness Inspection Before the Puppy Arrives

No matter how busy you are or how carefully you follow the puppy-proofing checklist, the day before your puppy arrives, be sure to set aside an hour or two to double-check that everything is in place.

Initial Meeting

Review the rules in Chapter 5 with all family members the day of the dog's arrival and before the pup actually arrives. Place heavy emphasis on how to handle the Lhasa Apso, particularly the part about not picking up your newest family member. The puppy is already going to be in a state of shock, so don't compound that by literally taking the world out from under your Lhasa Apso's feet.

Keep in mind that Lhasa Apsos tend to be wary of strangers and aren't particularly fond of children. All of this will need to be kept in mind so that the family is careful about the first interaction. Everyone needs to be aware to let the dog start interactions; people should not be screaming, squealing, or being very noisy, as this can be a source of anxiety for the Lhasa Apso. People should not crowd the puppy.

Determine who is going to be responsible for the primary puppy care and for primary training. To teach younger children responsibility, a parent can pair with a child to manage the puppy's care. The child can be responsible for feeding the puppy and keeping the water bowl filled. Of course, a parent should oversee these tasks.

Picking up Your Puppy or Dog and the Ride Home

A good bit of planning and preparation goes into picking up your puppy, especially if you are going to the breeder's home. If possible, do this on a weekend or during a holiday weekend or season. This will allow you unrushed, quality time at home with your new puppy.

As tempting as it is to cuddle the puppy in your lap, it is safer and more comfortable for the puppy if you use a crate for the ride home; two adults should also be present for the ride. This is the time to start teaching your puppy that car trips are enjoyable. This means making sure that the crate is securely anchored; you don't want the crate to slide around while he is helplessly sitting inside.

- The crate should be anchored in the car for safety and should include a cushion. If you have a long trip, bring food and water for the puppy and plan to stop at different intervals. Do not put food and water in the crate; sloshing water can scare your puppy. You can cover the bottom of the crate with a towel or pee pad in case of accidents.

- Call the breeder before you start the trip to make sure everything is still on schedule.

- Arrange for the mother dog to leave her scent on a blanket to help make the puppy's transition more comfortable.

- Make sure the second adult will be on time so that the two of you can head to the pick-up destination.

- If you have other dogs, make sure all of the adults involved in the intro-duction process know what to do. They should know the time and place for that first neutral territory meeting.

- If you do not have other dogs, you can pick up your puppy and head straight home. If you have a trip that lasts more than a couple of hours, stop periodically so your puppy can stretch, exercise, drink, and use the bathroom. Keep your puppy away from other dogs until he has gotten all of his shots; you don't want him to be exposed to a dog that is carry-ing a disease that your puppy is not fully protected against.

At no point should your puppy be left alone in the car. If you have to use the restroom, either go before leaving the breeder's place, or if you have a long drive ahead of you, have at least one adult remain with the puppy during each stop.

If the puppy has never ridden in a car before, someone should give the puppy attention while the other person drives. The puppy will be in the crate, but someone can still provide comfort. The puppy will definitely be scared without his mom, siblings, or familiar people to console him. Having someone talk to the puppy will make it less of an ordeal for the little one.

Photo Courtesy of Sherry Suffolk

When you arrive home, immediately take the puppy outside to use the bathroom. Even if he had an accident in his crate, this is the time to start training your new family member where to use the bathroom.

The First Vet Visit and What to Expect

The first vet visit will establish a baseline for the puppy's health. This will also allow the vet to track your puppy's progress and monitor his health as he grows. In addition to providing a chance to ask questions and get advice, this initial assessment will give you more information about your puppy. It also creates an important rapport between your Lhasa Apso and the vet.

During the first veterinary visit, your pup won't know what to expect. Try to ease his anxiety; you want this first appointment to set a positive tone for all future visits. This will likely be trickier with an adult dog than with a puppy, so be prepared to soothe any nervousness.

The following is a list of several things that must be completed before the day of the appointment:

- Find out how early you need to arrive to complete the paperwork for the new patient.
- Find out if you should bring a stool sample for that first visit. If so, collect it the morning of the visit and make sure to take it with you.
- Bring the paperwork provided by the breeder or rescue organization for the vet to add to your dog's records.

Upon your arrival, your Lhasa Apso may want to meet the other pups and people in the office and will probably announce your arrival. Although you will need to be mindful, this is an opportunity to socialize the puppy and to create a positive experience with the vet. Before letting your puppy meet other animals, always ask the owner for permission and wait for approval.

Photo Courtesy of Janine Bunting

Most pets at the vet's office are likely to not be feeling well, which means they may not be very affable. You don't want a grumpy, older dog or a sick animal to nip or scare your puppy. Negative social experiences are situations your puppy will remember; they could make future visits to the vet something to dread. Nor do you want your puppy to be exposed to potential illnesses before he has had all of his shots.

Every vet is different, so you should call your vet ahead of that first visit to get an idea of everything that will be done. Odds are, you will need to bring documentation about your dog, so this can also serve as a reminder to get your paperwork together and ready to go with you and your newest family member when you go to the vet the first time.

Young puppies will need a series of shots. The vet may also request that you bring your dog's latest poop to check it for parasites. Chapter 16 provides more details on what to expect if parasites are detected in your dog's bowel movement.

Be prepared for the vet to ask about your dog's history, even though you just brought the Lhasa Apso home with you.

During the first visit, the vet will conduct an initial assessment of your Lhasa Apso. One of the most important things the vet will do is weigh your dog. This is something you are going to have to monitor for your dog's entire life, as you will want to ensure that your Lhasa Apso remains at a healthy weight. Keep a record of his weight so you can see how quickly your puppy is growing and to make sure you aren't overfeeding him. Ask your vet what is considered a healthy weight for every growth stage and record that as well.

The vet will set a date for the next group of shots, which will likely happen not too long after the initial visit. After your Lhasa Apso receives his vaccinations (detailed in Chapter 16), prepare for a couple of days of your puppy feeling under the weather.

The following are other checks the vet may make during that initial visit.

- Most vets will listen to your dog's heart and lungs to make sure there aren't any obvious problems.
- They will take your pup's temperature, so be prepared to help by calming your dog, as he's probably not going to be happy with this activity.
- Vets usually check a dog's ears, eyes, nose, paws, skin/coat, and genitals.
- They will do a longer check on the mouth and teeth to look for potential problems.
- They will do an initial check on the abdomen and lymph nodes.

If the vet does find a problem and recommends medication, take the time to ask questions and make sure you know what to do before you leave the office.

Crate and Other Preliminary Training

Contrary to what some people think, crates are a safe space for dogs. Crate training will also prepare your dog for occasions when you may have to board him, and he will be put in a crate if you ever travel on a plane.

Puppies younger than six months should not be left in a crate for hours at a time. Your Lhasa Apso will not be able to hold his bladder for very long, so you must make sure he has a way to get out and to go to the bathroom. If you adopt an adult Lhasa Apso that is not house-trained, you will need to follow the same rules. If you aren't sure about whether or not the dog is house-trained, it is best to treat the adult as a puppy until you are certain that your newest family member won't use the house as a bathroom.

Make sure the crate door is set so that it doesn't close on your dog during his initial sniff of the crate. You do not want your Lhasa Apso to be scared by the door as it is closing behind him; this could make him fearful of the crate in the future.

The following are some suggestions:

- Use a positive, cheerful voice as you let your Lhasa Apso sniff the crate for the first time. The first experience in the crate should be associated with excitement and positive emotions. Be sure your dog understands the crate is a good place. If you have a blanket from the puppy's mother, put it in the crate to help provide an extra sense of comfort.

- Drop a couple of treats into the crate if your canine seems reluctant to enter. Do NOT force your dog into the crate. If your dog refuses to go all the way inside the crate, that is perfectly fine. It has to be the dog's decision to enter, so it doesn't become a negative experience.

- For a week or two, feed your dog while he is in the crate. Besides keeping the food away from any other pets, this will create positive associations between your Lhasa Apso and the crate.
    - If your dog appears comfortable with the crate, put the food all the way at the back.
    - If not, place the food bowl in the front, then move it further back in the crate over time.

- Start closing the door once your dog appears to be eating comfortably in the crate. When the food is gone, open the crate door immediately.

- Leave the door closed for longer periods of time after your dog has finished eating. If your pup begins to whine, you know you have left your Lhasa Apso in the crate for too long.

- Crate your dog for longer periods of time once the dog shows no signs of discomfort while in the crate when eating. Train your Lhasa Apso to go into the crate by simply saying, "Crate" or "Bed." Then, praise your dog to let him know that he has done an excellent job.

Repeat these steps for several weeks until your dog seems comfortable in the crate. The regular repetition several times a day teaches your dog that the crate is not a punishment and everything is alright. Initially, you should do this while you are still at home or when you go out to get the mail. When you leave the room, and your puppy lasts half an hour without whining, you can leave the dog alone for longer periods of time. However, keep this alone time to no more than an hour in the beginning.

During the first few weeks, you should also begin to house-train your Lhasa Apso. Basic behavioral training is also vital from the start. However, wait until your Lhasa Apso has all of his vaccinations before taking your new puppy to structured training classes. Knowledgeable trainers will not accept puppies in their classes until a dog's first full round of shots is complete.

Chapters 10 and 11 provide a closer look at how to train your dog.

Photo Courtesy
of Ma. Hanna Katrice Cleofas

First Night Frights

"

A puppy on the first day can be a joy. A puppy on the first night can be a nightmare! Puppies on the first night away from their siblings tend to scream at the top of their lungs. This is understandable because they are now in a new home with new smells and they don't recognize anything. The important tip is to stay strong and ignore the cry. The puppy will get better and better as the week goes on. You may have to wake up a few times to take them out to potty, but in general do not give the puppy love and attention every time it cries and screams for you. That will train your Lhasa to know that you will come to it whenever it cries.

CHOO MICHAEL YANG
Yangchoo Lhasa Apso

"

That first night is going to be terrifying for your little Lhasa Apso puppy! As understandable as this may be, there is only so much comfort you can give your new family member. The more you respond to his cries and whimpering, the more he will learn negative behavior provides the desired results. You need to prepare for a balancing act—one that reassures the Lhasa Apso that he is safe while keeping him from associating crying with receiving attention from you.

Create a sleeping area for your puppy near where you sleep. The area should have the puppy's bed tucked safely into his crate. This will offer him a safe place to hide and a place where he will feel more comfortable in this strange new home. The entire area should be blocked off to be sure no one can get in (and the puppy can't get out) during the night. This sleeping area should also be close to where people sleep so that the puppy doesn't feel abandoned. If you were able to get a blanket or pillow that smells like the dog's mother, make sure that this is in your puppy's space. Consider adding a little white noise (like an old-fashioned alarm clock) to cover unfamiliar sounds that could scare your new pet.

Your puppy will make noises over the course of the night. Don't move the puppy away, even if the whimpering keeps you awake. Being moved away from people will only scare him more, reinforcing the feeling of anxiety. When your puppy whines during the night, he is not whimpering because he's been in the crate too long. He's scared or wants someone to be with him—he's probably never been alone at night before coming to live with you. Spare yourself trouble later on by teaching the puppy that whimpering will not get him out of the crate. Over time, being close to you at night will be enough to reassure your puppy that everything will be fine.

In the beginning, puppies will need to go to the bathroom every two to three hours. This means you will also need to get up during the night! Make sure your puppy understands he must always go to the bathroom outside before bedtime or on the pee pad. If you ignore this rule, you will have a tough time training your dog to only relieve himself outside and not in the house.

HELPFUL TIP
Puppy Monitors

If your puppy will be sleeping in a room that's separate from your own, consider purchasing a set of baby monitors or video monitors to keep an eye on your pet during the night. Many modern monitors are compatible with smart phones and may be accessed via the internet, as well. A new dog or puppy might feel stressed in a new environment and may need extra company and reassurance during the first few weeks of transition.

If you choose to let your dog on the bed, wait until he is house-trained. Otherwise, you might have to replace your mattress within a short time. It is best to simply keep your Lhasa Apso off the furniture so that he doesn't get hurt and your furniture doesn't get ruined!

CHAPTER 8

Introducing Your Lhasa Apso to Your Other Dogs

Depending on the age of the dog, the initial introductions could be challenging. Lhasa Apso puppies tend to be easier to introduce than adult dogs, but you will want to take the same steps to introduce your new dog no matter how old they are. Nearly all dogs are hesitant initially when they meet another dog in a completely new environment. If you have other dogs, it is a chance to begin socializing your new Lhasa Apso (Chapter 12).

It is actually best if you have at least one other dog so that your Lhasa Apso isn't home alone while you are out shopping or at work. If you already have a socialized adult dog, your current dog can also help teach your new Lhasa Apso the rules, and he could even become a mentor to your puppy. If you adopt a puppy, he may imitate your current dog's obedience when you give directions, something that could be really helpful with a potentially stubborn breed. However, this works both ways. If your current dog displays negative behavior, you should try to correct these habits before your puppy arrives. You don't want your Lhasa Apso pup learning bad habits.

Introducing Your New Puppy to Your Other Pets

Introduce all new dogs to your current dog or dogs, regardless of age, in a neutral place away from your home. Even if you have never had problems with your current dog, you are about to change his world. When introducing your dog to the new puppy, select a park or other public area so your current dog will not feel territorial. This gives both animals the opportunity to meet and become familiar with each other on neutral ground.

When introducing the two dogs, make sure you have at least one other adult with you so that there's one person for each canine. All dogs should be leashed so that you can quickly and easily move them apart if the introduction does not go well. If you have more than two dogs, then you should have one adult per dog. This will make it easier to keep all of the dogs under control. Even the best dogs can get excited about meeting a puppy. One of the people who needs to be at this meeting is the person who is in charge of the pets in your home. This helps establish the pack hierarchy.

Don't hold your puppy in your arms when the dogs meet. While you may want to protect the puppy, holding him has the opposite effect. Instead, your puppy will feel trapped, but if the puppy is on the ground, he can run if he feels scared. Stand near the puppy with your feet a little bit apart, so the dog can hide behind your legs if he decides he needs to escape.

All dogs should have a few minutes to sniff each other, making sure there is always some slack in each leash. Feeling like they can move more freely helps dogs to relax, and they won't feel like you are trying to restrain them or force them into something. Your dog will either want to play, or he might simply ignore the puppy. You need to let your dog dictate what happens next. If the dogs want to play, be careful your current dog doesn't accidentally hurt the puppy, and if your dog ends up ignoring the puppy after an initial sniff, that is fine too. If your dog is clearly unhappy, keep all of the dogs apart until everyone is comfortable with the meeting. Don't force the situation.

Photo Courtesy of Tracy Kiely

Photo Courtesy
of Gary Furuyama

This introduction could take a while, depending on each individual dog's personality. The friendlier and more accepting your current dog is, the easier it will be to incorporate your new puppy into the home. For some dogs, a week is enough time to start feeling comfortable together. For other dogs, it could take a couple of months before they are fully accepting of a new puppy. Since this is a completely new dynamic for your dog, he may be angry with you for bringing this new bundle of energy into his life.

The older your current dog is, the more likely it is that a puppy will be an unwelcome addition. Older dogs can get cranky around a puppy who doesn't know when enough is enough! The goal is to make your puppy feel welcome and safe and to let your older dog know that your love for him is as strong as ever.

Once your new family member and the rest of the canine pack become acquainted and comfortable, you can head home. When you arrive, take the dogs into the yard and remove the leashes. Again, you will need one adult per dog, including the puppy. If the dogs are all right or are indifferent to the puppy, you can let your current dog inside. Then, re-leash the puppy, keeping him on the leash as you go inside.

Put the puppy in the puppy area when the introductions are complete. Remember to make sure your current dog cannot get into this area, and your puppy cannot get out.

Introducing an Adult Dog to Other Pets

Always approach the introduction (and first few weeks together) with caution. The new adult Lhasa Apso will need his own things from the very beginning—Lhasa Apsos can be territorial if not properly trained. When you aren't around, your dog should be kept in a separate area so there won't be any fighting among the dogs.

Plan for this introduction to take at least an hour. Since the dogs are both adults, they will need to move and become acquainted at their own pace.

When introducing your current dog(s) to your new dog, follow the same steps as you would with a puppy:

- Begin in neutral territory.
- Ask one adult to be present for each adult canine during the introduction.
- Introduce one dog at a time. Don't let several dogs meet your new Lhasa Apso all at once.

Bring treats to the meeting of two adult dogs—unlike with puppies. The animals will respond to the treats, and if the atmosphere becomes tense, the treats will create a distraction.

During the introduction, watch the Lhasa Apso and your dog(s) to see if any of them raise their hackles. This is one of the first obvious signs that a dog is uncomfortable. If the Lhasa Apso's hackles are up, back off the introductions for a little bit. Do this by calling your current dog back first.

FAMOUS LHASAS
Coco Chinetti

Coco Chinetti CGC TKE, a Lhasa Apso owned and trained by Sue Ridgley, is the first of his breed to be awarded the title of Trick Dog Elite Performer (TKE), the highest of five American Kennel Club (AKC) Trick Titles. When he was just a puppy, Coco attended puppy school for socialization and hid under his owner's chair for the first several weeks. After he came out of his shell and graduated puppy school, he went on to attend more formal training at Decatur Obedience Training Club. Coco has also earned the title Canine Good Citizen (CGC) through the AKC.

This is also when you should start waving treats around! Avoid pulling on the leashes to separate the dogs. You don't want to add physical tension to the situation because that could trigger a fight. Treats will work for all dogs, and calling their names should help get things under control.

If any of the dogs are showing their teeth or growling, call your dog back and give them a chance to settle down. Use treats and a calming voice to get them to relax. You want all the dogs to feel comfortable during the first meeting, so don't force the friendship. If they seem uncomfortable or wary at first, let them move at their own pace.

Older Dogs and Your Lhasa Apso

If your current dog is older, keep in mind puppies are energetic, and they want to engage older dogs in play. This can be very trying for your older canine, so make sure your older dog doesn't get too tired of the puppy's antics. A tired, older dog could snap and nip at your puppy in hopes of getting a little rest. You don't want your puppy to begin snapping at other dogs too. Watch for signs your older dog is ready for some alone time, some time with you, or simply a break from the puppy.

You should always make sure your older dog has safe places to be alone. This is essential for those times he just doesn't feel up to being around a spry, young puppy! By keeping your puppy and your older dog separate, you can prevent the need for constant scolding. Plus, the puppy will not become wary of older dogs.

Even if you rescue an adult Lhasa Apso, he might still be too energetic for your older dog to handle. Lhasa Apsos may be active dogs at any age! Be mindful and make sure your dog's golden years are not marred by a new canine that wants to play in a way your older dog can't. Lhasa Apsos are more likely to understand limits and boundaries faster than many other breeds, but you want to minimize how annoyed your older dog is while your puppy is learning those boundaries.

Dog Aggression and Territorial Behavior

Lhasa Apsos may exhibit a level of dominance or aggression toward dogs they don't know. This is one of the primary reasons why you should never let your Lhasa Apso off-leash. (Details on how to train your Lhasa Apso are discussed in Chapter 13.)

Dominance aggression is when your dog wants to show control over another animal or person. This kind of aggression can be seen in the following behaviors and in reaction to anyone going near the Lhasa Apso's belongings (like toys or a food bowl):

- Growling
- Nipping
- Snapping

Photo Courtesy
of Leonie Abram

Photo Courtesy of Ruth Close

This is the behavior that the pack leader uses to warn others not to touch their stuff. If you see this reaction in your Lhasa Apso while around you, a family member, or another pet, you must intervene immediately. Correct him by saying, "No," then lavish him with praise when the behavior stops. You must consistently intervene whenever your Lhasa Apso behaves in this manner.

Do not leave your Lhasa Apso alone with other people, dogs, or animals as long as any dominance aggression is exhibited. If you are not there to intervene, your dog will push boundaries and will likely try to show his dominance over those around him. Never train your Lhasa Apso to react aggressively!

Once you are sure this behavior has been eliminated, you can leave your current dog and Lhasa Apso alone for short periods of time. You should remain in another room or somewhere in close proximity but out of sight. Over time, you can leave your pets alone when you get the mail; then, try leaving them when you run errands or longer tasks. Eventually, you will be able to safely leave your Lhasa Apso alone with other dogs.

Feeding Time Practices

Your Lhasa Apso puppy will be fed in his puppy space, so mealtime will not be a problem in the beginning.

The following are suggestions for feeding your puppy when the other dogs are present; this will reduce the chance of territorial behavior:

- Feed your Lhasa Apso at the same time as the other dogs but in a different room. Keeping them separated will let your Lhasa Apso eat without distractions or feeling that your other dogs will eat what is in his bowl. Make sure to feed your Lhasa Apso in the same room each time while the other dogs eat in their established areas.

- Keep your Lhasa Apso and other dogs in their areas until they finish eating their food. Some dogs have a tendency to leave food in the bowl. Don't let them. They need to finish everything because all food bowls will be removed as soon as the dogs finish eating. If food is left, get the bowl off of the ground.

- Make sure you have someone near your Lhasa Apso so that the dog learns not to growl at people near the bowl. This will help reduce stress when other dogs are around the food. If your dog demonstrates any aggression, immediately correct him by saying, "No," then give praise when the behavior stops. Do not play with the food bowl, and make sure none of the kids play with it. Your dog needs to know that no one is going to try to steal his food.

- Over the course of a couple of weeks, move your dogs closer together while eating. For example, you can feed your current dog on one side of the door near the doorway and the Lhasa Apso on the opposite side.

- After a month or two, you can feed the dogs in the same room but with some distance between them. If your Lhasa Apso starts to exhibit protective behavior with the other dogs, correct the Lhasa Apso, then praise him when he stops the behavior.

Eventually, you can start feeding the dogs close to one another. This can take weeks to months to accomplish, depending on the age of the Lhasa Apso. A puppy will need less time because he will be socialized with the dogs from an early age, making him less wary. That does not mean he won't display territorial behavior. Yet, it likely won't take long for him to start to feel comfortable eating near the rest of the pack.

For adult dogs, this process could take longer, and you should not rush it. Let your dog learn to feel comfortable eating before you make changes, even small ones. Dogs of any breed can be protective of their food, depending on their past history. Before your dog will eat peacefully, he must be assured that his protective behavior is not necessary around other dogs. That means letting his confidence and comfort level build at his own pace.

CHAPTER 9

The First Few Weeks

The first few weeks with your new Lhasa Apso are going to be very emotional, especially as everyone learns how best to interact with your newest family member. Lhasa Apsos aren't particularly interested in exploring, but nearly every dog will want to look around its new home by the end of that first week. With their intelligence, Lhasa Apsos will likely quickly understand their new surroundings as they learn that this is their new home. When your dog is not sleeping, you may find yourself feeling that you can't get a moment's rest—but in a fun and entertaining way. The bond you and your Lhasa Apso form in those early days will be important in establishing the relationship you have over the years.

By the end of the first month, your pup should be sleeping through the night. House-training can be very easy when done right, but without the

Photo Courtesy of Jan-Maree Murphy

right approach, it can be a real chore. Having a great breeder who starts the process will further speed up how quickly your little one learns. You will want to monitor your Lhasa Apso, though, and never let a puppy or dog out of the dedicated area alone during that first week, and probably a good bit longer.

The first month is when you really need to start paying attention to your puppy's emerging personality. As with all intelligent breeds, the key is to remain consistent when it comes to training. That means everyone should be consistent, including the kids. Always use what you learn about your puppy's personality to encourage good behavior!

Setting the Rules and Sticking to Them

> "
> *It is important to set boundaries and limitations when adding a new Lhasa to the home. Lhasas are a very smart breed in the sense that if you don't train them, they will train you. And when they learn to train you, that's when problems will arise. Resource guarding can be a huge issue along with separation anxiety. Start your Lhasa on basic house manners right away, or you will have a challenging pet to live with.*
>
> CHOO MICHAEL YANG
> *Yangchoo Lhasa Apso*
> "

This goes for both your dog and your kids, regardless of the age of the dog or child. You don't want your older children or teens undoing your hard work by letting the new Lhasa Apso out of the puppy's dedicated area to roam. Make sure everyone knows that the rules apply to everyone.

Your puppy needs to understand the rules and to know you and your family mean them, even if the dog really doesn't like what you are saying. Once your canine learns to follow your commands, there will still be times when he will refuse to obey. That is nearly a certainty. However, he will be much more likely to listen when he knows you are in control.

Do not allow yourself or anyone in your family to think that making an exception is all right, no matter how cute those eyes are. Once a Lhasa Apso realizes that certain rules are negotiable, it will be incredibly difficult to teach him. The best reward is positive reinforcement, not breaking the rules.

Establish a No Jumping and No Mouthing Policy

If not properly trained, a Lhasa Apso may jump on you in greeting, and this can be very bad if the dog tries to jump on little children. Such a sturdy build can easily knock over a toddler without meaning to do it. You have the responsibility to ensure that your dog and children learn how to play properly. For your Lhasa Apso, this means no jumping on people. Any games that involve biting or nipping should always be avoided. You do not want your Lhasa Apso to ever think that nipping is all right. This will be very difficult if you don't enforce the rule right from the beginning.

NIPPING

Lhasa Apsos (or any dog) are likely to nip under two conditions. Most situations where dogs nip are related to these two scenarios.

- One of the triggers for nipping is overstimulation. This can be one sign your puppy is too tired to keep playing or training, and you should put him to bed.

- Another trigger could be that your canine has too much energy. If this is the case, take your puppy outside to burn off some of his excess energy. At the same time, be careful not to over exercise the puppy.

You need to be vigilant and immediately let your puppy know nipping is not acceptable. Some people recommend using a water spritzer bottle and spraying the puppy while saying, "No," after nipping. This is one of the few times when punishment may be effective, and it is probably essential. Remember—make sure your dog does not associate the spraying with anything other than his nipping. He needs to understand that he is getting sprayed because he is nipping someone and that this is not acceptable behavior.

Always firmly tell your puppy, "No," whenever he is

DID YOU KNOW?
How Big Will My Puppy Get?

Lhasa Apsos are a small breed and typically grow to be 10–11 inches tall and weigh between 12 and 18 pounds. Your puppy will most likely reach its full size around nine to 12 months, but this can take up to 18 months for some dogs. Male Lhasa Apsos tend to be larger than their female counterparts, weighing closer to the 18-pound side of the size range, while females tend to be closer to 12. A great way to anticipate your dog's full size is to look at its parents' sizes!

nipping, even if it is during playtime. You should also pull away and loudly say, "Ouch!" to let your puppy know his teeth are hurting you. This will help to establish the idea that nipping is bad and is never rewarded.

CHEWING

All puppies chew to relieve the pain of teething. Whether your dog is chewing on your furniture, utensils, or clothing, be sure to discourage this behavior as quickly as possible:

Photo Courtesy of Bianca Chad

- Make sure you have toys for your Lhasa Apso (whether an adult or a puppy) so that you can teach him what objects are acceptable for chewing. Having a lot of available toys and rotating those toys out will give your puppy or dog several options.

- If your puppy is teething, either refrigerate a couple of toys so that they are cold or give your puppy frozen carrots. The cold will help to numb the pain. Teething usually starts at between three and four months old, and it usually ends by eight months. You want to get toys that will be safe for his teeth in case your Lhasa Apso has problems. Chapter 13 also provides details on diets that may help dogs with allergies, such as a raw diet.

- Toys that are made either of hard rubber or hard nylon are best, particularly Kongs with kibble in them. You can even fill them with water and freeze them, which will give your puppy something cool to soothe the pain of teething.

For the most part, keeping an eye on your dog when he is not in his designated space will help you quickly see when he is chewing on things he shouldn't. When this happens, firmly say, "No." If your dog continues to chew, put him back in his space. While he is in the space, make sure he has plenty of toys to chew on.

If you decide to use chew deterrents, such as bitter training sprays, be aware some dogs will not care if an item tastes bad—they will chew on it anyway. If you apply these deterrents, do not leave your dog alone and expect him to stop chewing. You should watch your dog's reaction before trusting that the bad habit is broken. Since some Lhasa Apsos have separation anxiety, you should eliminate the chewing problem as quickly as possible; this will allow your pup to roam freely around your home.

Photo Courtesy
of Rod Timmis and Janette Humphreys

JUMPING

As noted earlier, even though they are small, Lhasa Apsos shouldn't be allowed to jump up on other people or animals. Use the following steps when you have a visitor. If you can, get someone who is willing to help because that will make training that much easier:

1. Put a leash on the dog when the person knocks on the door or rings the bell. The arrival of someone will invariably excite most dogs, especially puppies.

2. Let the person in, but do not approach the visitor until your pup calms down.

3. Be effusive in your praise when the puppy keeps all four paws on the ground.

4. If the puppy jumps up on the visitor, the visitor should turn his body and ignore the dog. Don't verbally correct the dog. Being completely ignored will be far more of a deterrent than any words you can say.

5. Give your dog something to hold in his mouth if he does not settle down. Sometimes dogs just need a task to reduce their excitement. A stuffed animal or a ball is an ideal distraction, even if your dog drops it.

6. At this point, the visitor can get low and pet your dog. Having someone on his level will make your Lhasa Apso feel he is being included. It also lets him sniff the visitor's face, which is part of a proper greeting to a dog. If your visitor is willing to help, this acknowledgment can prevent your pup from further jumping since he already feels safe with the person who is at his level.

Attention Seeking and Barking

If you are ignoring your Lhasa Apso, he may act like toddlers and young children do, resorting to any means of getting your attention, even if that attention is negative. There can be different ways of acting out, like destroying something or barking. Since what he really wants is your attention, the best way to train him is by ignoring him when he acts out. If he is barking, don't acknowledge him. Once he stops barking, count to five, then praise your Lhasa Apso for the quiet. If he destroys things, remove the items so he can do no harm.

Ignoring your dog is what works best for deterring attention-seeking behavior. As difficult as that may be, it is necessary to keep your puppy from

Photo Courtesy of Jackie Reynolds

learning how to push your buttons. After all, you do not want those behaviors to escalate when he is an adult. He will be able to do a lot more damage when he is older, and his voice will be a lot louder!

If you want to train your Lhasa Apso to be a watchdog, you won't want to entirely discourage barking. You simply want to train him not to bark for attention just because he is bored.

Reward-Based Training Versus Discipline-Based Training

With an intelligent breed like the Lhasa Apso, it is much more efficient to train your puppy using rewards than with punishments. This will be a particular challenge as puppies can be exuberant and are easily distracted. It is important to remember that your puppy is young, so you need to keep your temper and learn when a break from training is needed.

The following lists several critical training aspects you will need to address during the first month:

- House-training (Chapter 9)
- Crate training (Chapter 6)
- Barking (Chapter 11)

Find out how much house-training was completed by the breeder. The best breeders may teach puppies one or two commands before the puppy goes home with you. If this is the case, keep using those same commands with your puppy so that the early training is not lost. This information can help you establish the right tone of voice to use with your puppy since he will already know what the words mean and how to react to them.

How Long Is Too Long to Be Left Home Alone?

In the beginning, your dog should spend only a brief period of time in the crate while you are gone. Though Lhasa Apsos are often independent, they are still pack animals. They do better when they have their pack than when they are left home alone for lengthy periods of time. Also, in those early days, your home is a new, potentially scary place.

As your dog becomes house-trained and trustworthy, you should allow him to leave the crate while you are gone so that he doesn't feel he is being punished. Your new companion will not do well trapped in a crate for hours at a time.

You also need to find some good mental games that will keep your pup occupied while you are gone. Brain games can keep your dog happily occupied while you are away, and having another dog can provide stimulation (though you may want to make sure to tire them both out before leaving).

If you are gone for several hours most days of the week, you should have a second dog to keep the Lhasa Apso company. However, nothing is quite as good as having someone home most of the day. Work to overlap your day so that your Lhasa Apso has someone to hang out with.

Don't Overdo It – Physically or Mentally

As an adult, your Lhasa Apso will probably be highly active. As a puppy, your Lhasa Apso will go from sleeping to being rambunctious to sleeping again, all within a brief period of time. A tired puppy is a lot like a tired toddler; you have to keep the little guy from becoming exhausted or from overworking those little legs. You need to be careful about harming your puppy's growing bones. Your pup is probably going to think that sleep is unnecessary, no matter how tired he is. It is up to you to read the signs that tell you when to stop all activities and take a break or put your pup to bed.

You should train your dog in increments of time—only for the amount of time that he can handle. Don't push your puppy's training past his concentration level, and don't discourage your adult dog by using commands that are too advanced. If you continue training your puppy past his energy levels, the lessons learned are not going to be the ones you want to teach your dog. At this age, training sessions don't need to be long; they just need to be consistent.

Walks will be much shorter during the first month. When you go outside, stay within a few blocks of home. Don't worry—by the month's end,

Photo Courtesy of Betty Umaly

your puppy will have more stamina, and you can enjoy longer walks with your new friend. You can also do a bit of walking on the leash in the yard if your puppy has lots of extra energy. Puppies have a tendency to attack their leash while walking because it is a distraction from running freely. Taking walks will also help your Lhasa Apso learn how to behave on the leash.

Just because your puppy can't endure long walks initially doesn't mean he won't have plenty of energy. Daily exercise will be essential, with the caveats that you need to make sure your puppy isn't doing too much too soon and that he doesn't get too hot. Staying active will not only keep him healthy, but it will also keep him mentally stimulated. You will quickly realize how sedentary your "non-puppy life" has been because you will be on the move the entire time your puppy is awake!

Photo Courtesy of Xianne Aguiar

PART 3
TRAINING AND ACTIVITIES

CHAPTER 10
House-training

The recommended age to start trying to house-train a Lhasa Apso is between eight and 12 weeks. While you are trying to train the dog where to use the bathroom, you will probably start to see his mischievous side come out. This will make it harder to train him because you are more likely to be entertained than focused, which your dog is intelligent enough to notice. Getting you to lose your focus while getting to do what he wants to do is a win-win for your dog. All it takes is one time where you allow yourself to be distracted, and you can turn house-training into an incredibly difficult chore. Lhasa Apsos can be trained without a whole lot of trouble; it really comes down to how you complete the training.

Staying focused when you have your dog out for a restroom break isn't necessarily enough: if you fail to keep a constant eye on your puppy when he is exploring inside your home, be prepared for a lot of messes. Puppies will sneak off to use the bathroom inside if you let your attention stray. Lhasa Apsos can be stubborn, so you cannot give them any chance to get away with using your home as a bathroom.

Photo Courtesy of Ellie Knox

Photo Courtesy
of Deidre Wheatley

This is where learning to be firm and consistent is really going to count, and sticking to the rules will be absolutely essential. You will also need to remain calm and patient; getting upset will only reinforce undesirable behavior. The best tool in house-training a potentially stubborn breed is to set a schedule and stick to it—no deviations! Once your dog realizes you are staying focused and that you will get him outside for that break, he will accept that rule and do what he's supposed to do.

Leashing your Lhasa Apso to go outside can help show your puppy where and when to go to the bathroom – even in your yard. However, there will still be challenges.

The following is a list of rules to apply when house-training:

- Never let the puppy roam the house alone—he should always be in his dedicated puppy space when you are not watching him. No Lhasa Apso wants to spend a lot of time in a soiled crate, so being in his crate is a deterrent from doing his business there when you are not around. He may not feel the same way about other areas of your home if he is free to wander.

- Give your puppy constant, easy access to his designated bathroom spaces. You will need to make frequent trips outside with your puppy as he learns where to do his business.

- When you go outside, put a leash on your puppy to make a point of where in the yard you want him to use the bathroom.

Always begin with a training plan; then, be even stricter with yourself than you are with your puppy when keeping the schedule. You are the key to your puppy's learning!

Inside or Outside – House-training Options and Considerations

> "
>
> *Know the dogs patterns. If it is asleep and wakes up, it will need to go out. If playing, every 30 minutes take it out. Go out several times a day the first couple of days so the dog knows where the door is. Pay attention because they don't always bark. They may just stand in front of the door and stare at it. I actually had a puppy buyer teach them to ring a band of jingle bells by the door.*
>
> CARLA VARNEY
> *Hi Tide Lhasa Apsos*
>
> "

If your breeder has already started the house-training process, make sure to coordinate your training so that you pick up where they left off. Having someone who really knows how to house-train a dog can give you a huge leg up on the whole endeavor—take it if you can get it!

The following is a list of house-training options for your puppy:

- Pee pads – You should have several around the home for training, including in the puppy's area but as far from his bed as possible.

- Regular outings – Organize these outings based on your puppy's sleeping and eating schedule.

- Rewards – You can use treats in the beginning but quickly shift to praise.

Setting a Schedule

You need to keep an eye on your puppy and always follow his meals and sleep with house-training sessions. Watch for cues like sniffing and circling, which are two common signs a puppy exhibits when searching for a place to go. Start tailoring your schedule around your puppy's unique needs.

Puppies have small bladders and little control in the early days—so at this time, it isn't stubbornness but ability that is making it difficult for your puppy to follow your directions. If you train your pup to do his business inside, you need a designated space in the puppy's area for a clean pee pad. Make sure you change the pads regularly so that your puppy does not get accustomed to having waste nearby. Pee pads are better than newspapers and can absorb more. Even if you use pee pads, you should plan to transition your dog to doing his business outdoors as quickly as possible.

Choosing a Location

A designated bathroom space will make the house-training experience easier because your Lhasa Apso will associate one area of the yard with that specific purpose. Having him use one spot every time will also make cleanup simpler, and you will be able to use the entire yard instead of having to worry about stepping in dog waste.

The perfect time to train your puppy to go to the bathroom is when you go out for walks. Between walks and using the yard, your puppy will come to see the leash as a sign that it is time to relieve his bladder, which could become a Pavlovian response.

Do not send your puppy outside alone and assume he has done what you want him to do. He needs to understand the purpose of going outside is to go to the bathroom. Until there are no more accidents in the house, you need to be sure your puppy is not losing focus. With a breed like the Lhasa Apso, it is best to always verify that your little fellow follows through. If it is too hot or cold outside, and you don't make sure he takes care of business, you run the risk that he will take advantage of that lack of supervision to pretend just so he can get back inside faster. Then accidents are nearly guaranteed, even if you thought that your dog was fully house-trained.

Photo Courtesy of Deb Stover

Key Word Training

All training should include key words, even house-training. You and all family members should consistently use these key words when house-training your dog. If you have paired an adult with a child, the adult should be the one using the key word during training.

To avoid confusing your puppy, be careful not to select words that you often use inside the home. Use a phrase like, "Get busy," to let your puppy know it's time to do his business. Do not use words like "bathroom" or "potty" because these words are sometimes used in casual conversation, which could trigger a desire to go to the bathroom. "Get busy" is not a phrase most people use in their daily routine, so it is not something you are likely to say unless you want your puppy to go to the bathroom outside.

Photo Courtesy of Jamie Fensterstock

Once your puppy learns to use the bathroom based on the command, make sure he finishes before offering praise or rewards.

Reward Good Behavior with Positive Reinforcement

Carefully observe puppy to learn his "cues" that he is about to go so puppy can quickly be taken outside and an accident avoided. Always reward with a happy voice and a happy smile when he does his business outside. Praising a puppy for doing the right thing works best for everything you will do in life together. Make him think he is a little canine Einstein each time he performs this simple natural act. By developing good habits as a youngster puppy will have the basics needed for when he's really old enough to have better control.

KATHLEEN WALCOTT
Floral Hill Lhasa Apsos

Photo Courtesy
of Suzy Kelly

Lhasa Apsos are incredibly receptive to positive reinforcement, making it highly effective for all kinds of training (not just house-training). In the beginning, take a few pieces of kibble with you when you are teaching your puppy where to go, both inside and outside the home. Learning you are the one in charge will help teach your Lhasa Apso to look to you for cues and instructions.

Part of being consistent with training means lavishing the little guy with praise whenever your puppy does the right thing. Use a leash to gently lead your puppy to his bathroom area, with no stops in between. It will gradually become obvious to your Lhasa Apso that this is where he should go to use the bathroom. Once you get outside, encourage your pup to go only when you get to the place in the yard that is intended for his bathroom spot. As soon as he does his business, give him immediate and very enthusiastic praise. Pet your puppy as you talk, and let the little guy know just how good the action was. Once the praise is done, return inside immediately. This is not playtime. You want your puppy to associate certain outings with designated potty time.

HELPFUL TIP
Mess-Free Car Trips

Whether it's nerves or lack of house-training, some dogs tend to have more accidents while riding in the car. There are a number of options to help with this. If your dog rides in a crate in the car, line it with puppy pads or absorbent towels (pack a few extra if it will be a longer trip!). If your dog rides with a seat belt, look for dog diapers at your local pet store or online. Dog diapers come in a variety of sizes and styles, so choose the appropriate fit for your dog to avoid leaking.

While praise is incredibly effective with Lhasa Apsos, you can also give your puppy a treat after a few successful trips outside. Definitely do not make treats a habit after each trip because you do not want your Lhasa Apso to expect one every time he does his business. The lesson is to go outside, not to receive a treat every time.

The best way to house-train in the first couple of months is to go out every hour or two, even during the night. Set an alarm to wake yourself during the night so that you remember to take the puppy outside. Use the leash to keep the focus on using the bathroom, give the same enthusiastic praise, then immediately return inside and go back to bed. It is difficult, but your Lhasa Apso will get the hang of it a lot faster if there isn't a lengthy period between potty breaks. Over time, the pup will need to go outside less frequently.

Photo Courtesy
of Robynn Amaba

Cleaning Up

Once a dog goes to the bathroom in your home, that odor will remain there for other dogs to smell, even if it's not detectable to your own nose after you've cleaned the area thoroughly. Your Lhasa Apso might take any lingering odor as a sign that the spot is an acceptable place to use the bathroom.

This means you have to be very diligent about handling accidents:

- Clean up any messes in the house as soon as you find them.
- In areas where your dog has an accident, thoroughly clean the spot so that there is no remaining scent.

Spend a bit of time researching what kinds of cleaner you want to use, whether generic or holistic. For example, you will probably want to get a product with an enzyme cleaner. Enzymes help to remove stains by speeding up the chemical reaction of the cleaner with the stain. They also help to remove the smell faster, which reduces the odds your dog will continue to go to the bathroom in the same place. If your Lhasa Apso is properly trained, he will feel no need to mark his territory, but you should also discourage other dogs from claiming areas around your property.

If your Lhasa Apso has an accident, it is important to refrain from punishing the puppy. Punishment simply teaches your dog to hide his mess or to be stealthier about when he does his business inside. Accidents are not a reason to punish. If they happen often, it is really more of a reflection of your training and your schedule than on the puppy. However, even the best trainers can tell you accidents are pretty much an inevitability. When it happens, tell your puppy, "No! Potty outside!" and clean up the mess immediately. Once you have finished cleaning the mess, take the puppy outside. It isn't likely that he will need to go potty again, but it is worth the attempt in case he still has a little left.

Pay attention to when these accidents happen, and determine if there is a commonality between them. Perhaps you need to add an extra trip outside during the day for your puppy, or you should make a change in his walking schedule. Maybe there is something that is startling your dog and causing an accident.

CHAPTER 11
Training Your Lhasa Apso

> "
>
> *Lhasas are extremely intelligent. Often they are called stubborn, but actually they are deep thinkers who only obey when what they are asked to do makes sense (is fun or rewarding) to them. So for training to be effective it must always be positive, fun, and reward- ing; never harsh or demanding in nature. Training with patience and understanding can be very rewarding as a Lhasa wants very much to please those they love.*
>
> KATHLEEN WALCOTT
> *Floral Hill Lhasa Apsos*
>
> "

If you ask the Lhasa Apso community if this is a dog that's easy to train, you are going to get a lot of different responses, and they are all right. As independent dogs, Lhasa Apsos aren't always receptive to training. This isn't a breed that prioritizes your happiness over their convenience, and that is exactly what you need to keep in mind when you start training your dog. Make training something your puppy enjoys, and he can learn very quickly.

If you have a puppy, getting started early can make this task a lot easier. Older dogs that aren't accustomed to training will be a lot more challenging, but this doesn't mean that they can't be persuaded to follow at least the basic commands.

It is absolutely essential to ensure that your Lhasa Apso learns the basic commands covered in these chapters for his own protection. Given their size, a Lhasa Apso can slip away easily, and that can be incredibly danger- ous for him. If you find that you are having a lot of problems, the end of this chapter provides details about the kinds of classes you can enroll your Lhasa Apso in to make sure he learns to listen for the basic commands.

With the right incentives, most dogs get over that stubborn streak because they would much rather have fun with you than just get their way. When weighing what they want against play, Lhasa Apsos are more interested in having fun – you just need to be able to persuade them that listening is more fun than making their own fun.

Best Practices and Benefits to Keep in Mind before You Start

In the early days, be prepared to keep your frustration levels in check. Your dog has to be convinced of the idea that you are in charge and that you mean business—and he needs to know the reward for that is a lot of fun. If you take out your frustration on your Lhasa Apso, you are teaching him that training isn't fun. Whether you bring a puppy or an adult dog into the home, he has to learn the boundaries in a way that is safe and shows patience, just like with teaching a child. If you take a few minutes to watch training videos of Lhasa Apsos from the beginning, that will give you a good idea of what you could be in for when you start to train your newest family member.

Just remember—being firm, consistent, and patient will go a long way. Don't let that adorable face sway you from getting your pup to do what you instruct him to do. Remember, he will be just as happy a little way down the

HELPFUL TIP
Training Treats

Lhasa Apsos have a bit of a reputation for being stubborn and difficult to train. Still, early socialization and training can go a long way toward raising a well-adjusted dog of any breed. Positive reinforcement is a great way to reward your Lhasa Apso for positive behavior. Keep a bag of training treats, or a handful of kibble, to reward your dog each time he's doing something you want him to continue. Since Lhasa Apsos aren't large dogs, it's essential to stick to small treats that can be eaten quickly when choosing your training treats.

road if you stick to it now. And that happy face when playing with you is priceless.

Always make the early training sessions short, no matter how old your dog is. Those training sessions are as much about learning how your Lhasa Apso will respond to training as they are about actually training. Puppies won't have the ability to keep focus like an adult, so a short session is ideal for keeping them from learning to ignore you. Adult dogs are going to be suspicious of you (though you may also get an adult that is already familiar with training, which could make training a little easier). And odds are, you are going to be quite tired by the end of those sessions—you'll be just as relieved as your pup to be done. As long as you are firm and consistent during those early sessions, keeping them short is in everyone's best interest.

Training will be slow going in the beginning as your dog will be quite excited about the interaction. Don't take this as an indication of your puppy's interest levels—it's more indicative of his inexperience. If you are patient with your pup from the start, you will find it will pay off later.

Training is as important as socialization, and it can make general excursions easier; more importantly, training could be a way of saving your dog's life. Understanding commands might prevent your dog from running into the street, from responding to provocations from other dogs, or from acting territorial.

Training can also really benefit your relationship with your pup because it is a wonderful way to bond. This dedicated time together helps you understand your puppy's developing personality as you learn what kind of reward will work best for other tasks. Be sure your Lhasa Apso is well-trained so you can enjoy a full range of activities together—from picnics to outings in the park!

Choosing the Right Reward

The right reward for a Lhasa Apso will ultimately be love and affection because they adore their people. Treats are the easiest way of keying a puppy into the idea that performing tricks is good behavior, but ultimately you want your little one to follow commands without expecting food. Soon, you will need to switch to a reward that is a secondary reinforcer. Praise, additional playtime, and extra petting are all fantastic rewards for your Lhasa Apso. Your dog will probably follow you around until you decide to just sit back and relax. Plopping down to watch a movie and letting your puppy sit with you is a great reward after an intense training session. Not only did your puppy learn, but you both now get to relax together.

Because this is a smaller breed, you need to be careful about overfeeding your dog, and that includes treats. Make sure you switch to a different kind of positive reward as early as possible. Since many Lhasa Apsos love their toys, you don't have to rely solely on treats as a method of praise.

If you would like your Lhasa Apso to connect positive feedback with a sound, you can use a clicker. This training tool is relatively inexpensive and should be used at the same time as you praise your puppy or dog. Clickers are not necessary, but some trainers find them useful.

Name Recognition

Over time, many of us create different names for our dogs. Nicknames, joke names, and descriptions based on some of their ridiculous actions can all be used later. However, before you can train a dog, you have to make sure he understands his real name.

The following list gives some name recognition suggestions:

1. Get some treats and show one to your dog.
2. Say the dog's name and immediately say, "Yes." (Your dog should be looking at you when you speak.) Then, give your dog a treat.
3. Wait 10 seconds, then show your dog a treat and repeat step two.

Sessions shouldn't last longer than about five minutes because your dog will lose focus or interest. Name recognition is something you can do several times each day. After you have done this for five to 10 sessions, the training will change a bit:

1. Wait until your dog isn't paying attention to you.

2. Call your dog. If he has a leash on, give it a gentle tug to get your dog's attention.

3. Say, "Yes," and give the dog a treat when he looks at you.

During this time, do not speak your dog's name when you correct him or for any reason other than name recognition. This is because, in the beginning, you need to get the dog to associate his name only with something positive, like treats. This will more quickly program your dog to listen to you no matter what else is going on around him.

It is likely that your Lhasa Apso will not require a lot of time before he recognizes his name. Repetition while looking at your pup is a great way to speed up the learning process.

Essential Commands

There are six basic commands that all dogs should know (Sit, Down, Stay, Come, Leave It, and Drop It). These commands are the basis for a happy and enjoyable relationship with your dog, as well as giving you a way to keep your dog safe and out of trouble. Then there are some commands that are incredibly helpful, like Off if you don't want pets on the furniture and Quiet for a noisy dog.

Photo Courtesy of Izabela Sokolowska-Nowak

Train your puppy to do the commands in the order they appear in this chapter. The last two are optional since you may allow your dog on the furniture, and he may not be a particularly vocal canine. Since dogs sit often, it is the easiest command to teach, making it the best starting point. Teaching Leave It and Drop It are much more difficult and usually require the puppy to fight an instinct or a desire. Consider how often you give in to something you want, even when you know you shouldn't! That's pretty much what your puppy is facing.

Quiet can be another difficult command, as dogs (particularly puppies) tend to bark in response to their surroundings. However, you don't have to teach it right from the beginning, as some puppies do grow out of the constantly barking stage. If you finish all the other commands and find that your dog is still a bit too noisy for your home, you can then start training, though you will need to determine just when you want him to be quiet and when you want him to bark (like when someone is outside your home). This will take some consideration on your part before you begin.

The following are some basic steps to use during training:

1. Include everyone in the home in the Lhasa Apso training. The puppy must learn to listen to everyone in the household and not just one or two people. A set training schedule may only involve a couple of people in the beginning, especially if you have children. There should always be an adult present when training, but including a child will help reinforce the idea that the puppy must listen to everyone in the house. It is also an effective way for a parent to monitor a child's interaction with the puppy so that everyone plays in a way that is safe and that follows the rules.

2. To get started, select an area where you and your puppy have no other distractions, including noise. Leave your phone and other devices out of range so that you are able to keep your attention on the puppy.

3. Stay happy and excited about the training. Your puppy will pick up on your enthusiasm and will focus better because of it.

4. Be consistent and firm as you teach.

5. Bring special treats to the first few training sessions, such as pieces of chicken or small treats.

Sit

Start to teach the command Sit when your puppy is around eight weeks old.

Once you settle into your quiet training location:

1. Hold out a treat.

2. Move the treat over your puppy's head. This will make the puppy move back.

3. Say, "Sit" as the puppy's haunches touch the floor.

Having a second person around to demonstrate this with your puppy will be helpful, as the person can sit to show the dog what you mean.

Photo Courtesy
of Brittany Kerstetter

Wait until your puppy starts to sit down and say, "Sit" as he sits. If your puppy finishes sitting down, give praise. Naturally, this will make your puppy excited and wiggly, so it may take a bit of time before he will want to sit again. When your puppy calms down, repeat the process.

It's going to take more than a couple of sessions for the puppy to fully connect your words with the actions. Commands are something completely new to your little companion. Once your puppy has demonstrated mastery of the command Sit, start teaching Down.

Down

Repeat the same process when teaching this command as you did for Sit:

1. Tell your dog to Sit.
2. Hold out the treat.
3. Lower the treat to the floor with your dog sniffing at it. Allow your pup to lick the treat, but if he stands up, start over.

Say, "Down" as the puppy's elbows touch the floor (make sure to say it as he does the action to help him associate the word with the action), then give praise while rewarding your puppy with the treat.

It will probably take a little less time to teach this command. Wait until your puppy has mastered Down before moving on to Stay.

Stay

Stay is a vital command to teach because it can keep your puppy from running across a street or from running at someone who is nervous or scared of dogs. It is important your dog has mastered Sit and Down before you teach Stay. Learning this command is going to be more difficult since it is not something your puppy does naturally.

Be prepared for this command to take a bit longer to teach:

1. Tell your puppy to either Sit or Stay.

2. As you do this, place your hand in front of the puppy's face.

3. Wait until the puppy stops trying to lick your hand before you continue.

4. When the puppy settles down, take a step away. If your puppy is not moving, say, "Stay," and give a treat and some praise.

Photo Courtesy of Brittany Kerstetter

Giving your puppy the reward indicates the command is over, but you also need to indicate the command is complete. The puppy has to learn to stay until you say it is okay to leave the spot. Once you give the okay to move, do not give treats. The command Come should not be used as the okay word, as it is a command used for something else.

Repeat these steps, taking more steps further away from the puppy after a successful command.

Once your puppy understands Stay when you move away, start training him to Stay even if you are not moving. Extend the amount of time required for the puppy to stay in one spot so that he understands Stay ends with the Okay command.

When you feel that your puppy has Stay mastered, start training the puppy to Come.

Come

This is a command you can't teach until the puppy has learned the previous commands. Before you start the training session, decide if you want to use Come or Come Here. Be consistent in the words you use.

This command is important for the same reason as the previous one; if you are around people who are nervous around dogs, or if you encounter a wild animal or other distraction, this command will snap your puppy's attention back to you:

1. Leash the puppy.

2. Tell the puppy to Stay.

3. Move away from the puppy.

4. Say the command you will use for Come and give a gentle tug on the leash toward you.

Repeat these steps, building a larger distance between you and the puppy. Once the puppy seems to understand, remove the leash, and start at a close distance. If your puppy doesn't seem to understand the command, give some visual clues about what you want. For example, you can pat your leg or snap your fingers. As soon as your puppy comes running over to you, offer a reward.

Leave It

This is a difficult training command, but you need to train your dog to Leave It for when you are out on a walk and want him to ignore other people or dogs.

1. Let your dog see that you have treats in your hand, then close your hand. Your fist should be close enough for your dog to sniff the treat.

2. Say, "Leave it" when your dog starts to sniff your hand.

3. Say, "Yes," and give your dog a treat when he turns his head away from the treats. Initially, this will probably take a while, as your dog will want those treats. Don't continue to say, "Leave it," as your dog should not be learning that you will give a command more than once. You want him to learn he must do what you say the first time, which is why treats are recommended in the beginning. If a minute or more passes after giving the command, you can then issue it again, but make sure your canine is focused on you and not distracted.

These sessions should only last about five minutes. Your dog will need time to learn this command as you are teaching him to ignore something he does naturally. When he looks away and stops sniffing when you say, "Leave it," you can move on to more advanced versions of the training:

Photo Courtesy of Natalie Bond

1. Leave your hand open so that your dog can see the treats.

2. Say, "Leave it" when your dog starts to show interest. This will probably be immediate since your hand will be open, so be prepared.

🅐 Close your fist if your dog continues to sniff or gets near the treats in your hand.

🅑 Give your dog a treat from your other hand if he stops.

Repeat these steps until your dog finally stops trying to sniff the treats. When your dog seems to have learned this command, move on to the most difficult version of this command.

1. Place treats on the ground, or let your dog see you hide them. Then, stay close to those treats.

2. Say, "Leave it" when your dog starts to show interest in sniffing the treats.

🅐 Place a hand over the treats if he doesn't listen.

🅑 Give a treat if your dog does listen.

From here, you can start training while standing further from the treat with your dog leashed, so you can stop him if needed. Then, start to use other things that your dog loves, such as a favorite toy or another tempting treat that you don't usually give him.

Drop It

This is going to be one of the most difficult commands to teach because it goes against both your puppy's instincts and interests. Your puppy wants to keep whatever he has, so you are going to have to offer him something better instead. It is essential to teach the command early, as your Lhasa Apso could be very destructive in the early days. Furthermore, this command could save your pooch's life. When you are out for a walk, he will probably lunge at objects that look like food. However, once he has mastered this command, he will drop anything he picks up.

Start with a toy and a large treat that your dog cannot eat in a matter of seconds, such as a rawhide. Make sure the treat you have is one your puppy does not get very often so that there is motivation to drop the toy or big treat.

1. Give your puppy the toy or large treat. If you want to use a clicker, too, pair it with the exciting treat you will use to help convince your puppy to drop the treat.

2. Show your puppy the exciting treat.

3. Say, "Drop it," and when he drops the treat or toy, tell him, "Good," and hand over the exciting treat while picking up the dropped item.

4. Repeat this immediately after your puppy finishes eating the exciting treat.

You will need to keep reinforcing this command for months after it is learned because it is not a natural instinct.

Off

This is different from training your dog not to jump on people (Chapter 9). This command is specifically to get your dog off furniture or surfaces that may be dangerous. This is training you will need to do on the fly because you are training your dog to stop an action. This means you have to react to that undesirable action. Having treats on hand will be essential when you see your dog getting up on things you don't want him to be on:

1. Wait for your dog to put his paws on something you don't want him on.

2. Say, "Off," and lure him away with a treat that you keep just out of his reach.

3. Say, "Yes," and give him a treat as soon as his paws are off the surface.

Repeat this every time you see the behavior. It will probably take at least half a dozen times before your dog understands he should not perform the action anymore. Over time, switch from treats to praise or playing with a toy.

Quiet

Lhasa Apsos were originally bred to bark at intruders in temples or palaces, but you may want to train the pup not to bark too often. Initially, you can use treats sparingly to reinforce quiet if your pup enjoys making noise:

1. When your puppy barks for no obvious reason, tell him to be quiet and place a treat nearby. It is almost guaranteed your dog will fall silent to sniff the treat.

2. If your dog does fall silent, say, "Good dog" or "Good quiet."

It will not take too long for your puppy to understand Quiet means no barking.

If you want your Lhasa Apso to be more of a watchdog, you will need to provide some guidance on when he should bark and when he should not. He will likely bark at the door when someone is there, so it won't be as difficult to teach him to bark for other reasons as well. A professional can help tailor the approach to training your dog when to bark at people at the door. Otherwise, you will want your dog to know he shouldn't be randomly barking at birds at the window or squirrels running around in the yard.

Until all of these commands are learned, it is best to avoid other types of advanced training. Between six and twelve months, you should be able to move on to tricks. Chapter 14 provides more details on tricks and games that your Lhasa Apso may love.

Where to Go from Here

66

Lhasas will get bored very easily. If you go to obedience class make sure you don't do things too many times. If they are doing things well, don't keep repeating it. They will get bored and decide they have had enough. Always stop at a happy ending. If the dog is doing well, end that training while you are ahead.

CARLA VARNEY
Hi Tide Lhasa Apsos

99

Given the potential difficulty level for training a Lhasa Apso, if you find that you need help, there are several types of classes you can sign up for to get the help you need. If you have a puppy, you may want to consider enrolling him in a class as early as possible so that you can learn how best to approach training your potentially headstrong puppy.

Puppy Classes

Puppies can begin to go to puppy school as early as six weeks of age. You will need to set aside an hour or two so that you can research schools near you. Make sure to take the time to read the reviews and see if you can talk to people who have used a particular school or trainer. Trainers should be willing to take the time to talk to you and answer questions as well, so try talking to the people running the school. This is the beginning of obedience training, but you need to be careful around other dogs until your puppy has completed his vaccinations. Talk with your vet about when is an appropriate time to begin classes. Your vet may be able to recommend good puppy training classes in your area.

The primary purpose of these classes is socialization. Studies show one-third of all puppies have minimal exposure to unfamiliar people and dogs during the first 20 weeks of their life. This can make the outside world pretty scary! The puppy classes give you and your puppy a chance to learn how to meet and greet other people and dogs in a controlled environment. Dogs that attend these classes are much friendlier and are less stressed about such things as large trucks, thunder, loud noises, and unfamiliar visitors. They are also less likely to be nervous or suffer from separation anxiety, a likely issue for a Lhasa Apso.

Puppy classes are also great training for you! The same studies show owners who attend classes learn to react appropriately when their puppy is disobedient or misbehaves. The classes teach you how to train your puppy and how to deal with the emerging headstrong nature of your dog.

Many classes will help you with some of the basic commands, like Sit and Down. Look for a class that also focuses on socialization so that your puppy can get the most out of the instruction.

By the end of the class, you will probably already have an idea of how well your Lhasa Apso will respond to training. If you feel you still need support because your pup is still proving to be less interested in listening to you, obedience training will be a great next step.

Obedience Training

Dogs of nearly any age can attend obedience training classes, although your dog should be old enough to listen to commands before instruction begins. At this point, you will start to see just how much harder Lhasa Apsos can be to train over some of the other intelligent but people-pleasing dogs, like German Shepherds and Retrievers. It is best not to compare the progress between your dog and others. Remember, as long as your dog is learning, it doesn't matter that it takes a little longer. Once your Lhasa Apso recognizes that you are serious, he will probably accept it and will start to follow through with what you want.

Beyond teaching your dog to listen to you, obedience training provides the foundation for more serious training. Obedience training usually includes the following:

1. Teaching or reinforcing basic commands, like Sit, Stay, Come, and Down.

2. How to walk without pulling on the leash.

3. How to properly greet people and other dogs, including not jumping on them.

Obedience school is as much about training you as training your dog. It helps you learn how to train your puppy while teaching your dog basic commands and how to behave for basic tasks, like greetings and walking. Classes usually last between seven and 10 weeks.

Ask your vet for recommendations, and also consider the following when evaluating trainers:

- Are they certified, particularly the CPDT-KA certification?
- How many years have they been training dogs?
- Do they have experience with training Lhasa Apsos?
- Can you participate in the training? If the answer is no, do not use that trainer. You have to be a part of your dog's training because the trainer won't be around for most of your dog's life.

Therefore, your dog has to learn to listen to you.

If your dog has anxiety, depression, or other serious behavioral problems, you need to hire a trainer to help your dog work through those issues. Do your research to be sure your trainer is an expert—preferably one with experience training intelligent, strong-willed dogs.

Once your Lhasa Apso understands the basic commands and has done well in obedience training, you will know if more difficult training is right for him.

CHAPTER 12
Socialization

> "
>
> *Once your puppy's vaccinations are complete it is good to introduce them to friendly new people, calm, friendly dogs, pleasant sights and sounds so they will grow up with a confident personality. Taking a walk with a friendly neighbor and their well mannered dog can be a nice relaxing introduction to all kinds of new sights, sounds, smells. Never coerce your puppy to make new friends, but let them do it the Lhasa way, giving them the opportunity to assess the situation and then your puppy will approach a person, or dog, whom they decides could be a fun friend.*
>
> KATHLEEN WALCOTT
> *Floral Hill Lhasa Apsos*
>
> "

Socialization is essential for every dog. Without socialization, dogs tend to be more afraid or wary, which can result in unexpected aggression. Any dog with a history of being a watch or guard dog is more likely to be problematic when it comes to socialization if he isn't socialized from a very early age.

It is difficult to predict how well Lhasa Apsos will get along with others because some are very personable, and others are much more standoffish. The parents' temperament can be a good predictor of how affable your Lhasa Apso will be, but it isn't a guarantee. This is why it is absolutely essential to start socializing your new dog as soon as possible.

Socialization starts from the moment you pick up your Lhasa Apso, and it will continue over the rest of your Lhasa Apso's life. Create regular time in your schedule to ensure that your dog receives socialization to bring out those fantastic, mischievous personality traits that are built into his genetics. If you begin socialization when your puppy is still young, he will learn that other dogs and people can be a lot of fun. Remember that your puppy will need to have all of his vaccinations before being exposed to other dogs.

Photo Courtesy
of Choo Michael Yang

Another benefit of early socialization is that it can make life much more enjoyable for everyone involved, no matter what the situation. A socialized dog will approach the world from a much better place than a dog that is not socialized.

Keep in mind that Lhasa Apsos are not particularly patient, so be prepared for very close supervision with your dog and younger children. Kids may be too handsy for such an independent dog, so don't leave your Lhasa Apso alone with any children.

Greeting New People

Most puppies enjoy meeting new people. Make sure to invite friends over to help socialize your new canine family member. Your Lhasa Apso may initially react by barking when a new person appears, but this likely will stop as soon as the person tries to pet your pooch. Still, you will need to be careful to make sure that there are no territorial behaviors or excessive wariness.

The following is a list of methods to use when introducing your puppy to a new person:

- Try to have your puppy meet new people daily, if possible. This could be during walks or while you are doing other activities, both inside and outside of the house. If you can't meet new people daily, try to meet new people at least four times a week.

- Invite friends and family over and let them spend a few minutes giving the puppy their undivided attention. If your puppy has a favorite game or activity, let people know so they can play with him. This will win the little guy over very quickly and teach him new people are fun and safe to be around.

Photo Courtesy
of Natalie Riley

Photo Courtesy
of Katherine Miller

- Once your puppy is old enough to learn to do tricks (after the first month), have your little friend perform his tricks for visitors.

- Avoid crowds for the first few months. When your puppy is older, attend dog-friendly events so that your pup can learn to be comfortable around a large group of people.

Greeting New Dogs

Chapter 8 explained how to introduce your new Lhasa Apso to your other dogs. It is considerably different when meeting other dogs because it can happen more unexpectedly, such as when you go for a walk.

The first goal is to be able to walk around your neighborhood while your dog remains calm, refraining from running up to other dogs that may not be as friendly. The problem will probably be with the other dog, particularly if the other dog is not sociable; having a dog running toward it may be upsetting. Therefore, you need to train your Lhasa Apso to be calm around other dogs as early as possible to keep him safe.

Most dogs will bow and sniff each other during an introduction. Remember to watch for signs of aggression (Chapter 8), such as raised hackles and bared teeth. It is unlikely, but it is best to be safe. Bowing, hightail, and perked ears usually mean that your Lhasa Apso is excited about meeting the other dog. If your Lhasa Apso is making noises, make sure that the sounds are playful by paying attention to the physical reaction. This applies

DID YOU KNOW?
Prey Drive

Each dog breed has a unique level of prey drive inherent to their ancestry. Lhasa Apsos have a high prey drive in general, which means that they will instinctively chase small animals, such as rodents or small cats, and most love playing chase. Prey drive can be managed and mitigated with socialization and appropriate training. Work on your dog's recall and use positive reinforcement to redirect your dog from its prey.

more if you adopted an adult than if you have a puppy, but it is always a good idea to keep an eye out regardless of the age of your dog.

The best way to help a Lhasa Apso feel comfortable around unfamiliar dogs is to set up playdates with other dogs in a neutral place. This should make the whole experience much easier.

Don't let your Lhasa Apso jump up on other dogs, no matter how excited he is. This action can become a way of showing dominance, which you really don't want with your puppy, even if it is just play in the beginning. If he does jump up, immediately say, "No," to let him know it is not acceptable behavior.

The Importance of Continuing Socialization

To keep your Lhasa Apso from turning into a little curmudgeon, you need to keep up with socialization. When family and friends visit, encourage them to bring their dogs. This will remind your Lhasa Apso his home is a welcoming place and not somewhere he needs to exert his dominance. You do not want your dog to think he can be a terror in his own house.

Socializing an Adult Dog

Socializing an adult canine requires a lot of time, dedication, gentle training, and a firm approach. There's no guarantee that your dog will be happy being around other dogs. You may be lucky enough to get an adult that is already well-socialized. That does not mean you can remain entirely relaxed! Your new dog may have had a terrible experience with a particular breed of dog that no one knows about, and this can result in a bad situation.

Your dog should be adept at the following commands before you work on socialization:

Photo Courtesy of Toni Burgess

- Sit
- Down
- Heel
- Stay

"Stay" is especially important because this demonstrates your dog has self-control by remaining in one place based on your command. This quality will be helpful when socializing because using this command will allow you to control your Lhasa Apso in any situation. When you go outside, you will need to be very aware of your surroundings and be able to command your dog before another dog or person gets near him.

Photo Courtesy
of Icey Vallesteros

- Use a short leash on walks. Being aware of your surroundings will start to cue you in to what is making your dog react, so you can start training him not to react negatively.

- Change direction if you notice your Lhasa Apso is not reacting well to a person or dog that is approaching. Avoidance is a good short-term solution until you know your dog is more accepting of the presence of other dogs or people.

- If you are not able to take a different direction, tell your dog to sit, then block his view. This can prove to be particularly challenging, as he will try to look around you. Continue to distract your dog so he will listen to you, taking his mind off what is coming toward him.

- Ask friends with friendly dogs to visit you, then meet in an enclosed space. Having one or two friendly dogs to interact with can help your Lhasa Apso realize not all dogs are dangerous or need to be put in their place. When dogs wander around the area together, with no real interaction, your dog will learn that the others are enjoying the outside too. So, there is no reason to try to bully them!

- Get special treats for when you go walking. If your dog is aggressive when walking, have him sit and give him one of the special treats. Lhasa Apsos are food motivated, so this could be a perfect way of distracting your dog from whatever is making him feel protective. At the first snarl or sign of aggression, engage the training mentality and draw upon your dog's desire for those special treats. This method is slow, but it is reliable because your dog will learn that the appearance of strangers and other dogs means special treats for him. He will realize going on a walk is a positive experience and not a negative one. Nonetheless, this does not train him to interact with those dogs. Couple this tip with the previous suggestion to get the best results.

Photo Courtesy of Jenna Davies

If you have ongoing problems with your adult dog, consult a behaviorist or specialized trainer.

CHAPTER 13
Playtime and Exercise

Lhasa Apsos aren't particularly energetic, but their intelligence does mean you need to tire them out to keep them from getting into trouble. When done right, playtime can actually be great to help your Lhasa Apso and children to bond.

There are plenty of other benefits to ensuring your Lhasa Apso gets adequate activity every day:

- It helps keep your dog at a healthier weight.
- He will be tired enough not to be too much trouble, especially if you need to leave him alone for a little while.
- Playtime is great for family bonding, as well as bonding with your dog.

On cold and rainy days, it is still pretty easy to ensure your Lhasa Apso gets adequate exercise because of how small he is. Still, getting outside for a bit of exercise daily is best for you and your dog.

Photo Courtesy of Choo Michael Yang

Exercise Needs

> *They say that a tired dog is a happy dog. Depending on the energy level of your Lhasa, an owner should exercise their dog accordingly to have a well balanced house dog. A high energy Lhasa could benefit from a walk or light jog. Lhasas also excel in agility and other dog competitions. Exercising a dog mentally also makes a dog tired. It makes them use their brain and by the end of training, they're tired just like how humans are tired after a long day at the office. A good enrichment to exercise the brain is something like training on nose work, where the dog will find a scent and get a reward. Just know your dog's limit and keep everything fun for them.*
>
> CHOO MICHAEL YANG
> *Yangchoo Lhasa Apso*

A good 30-minute brisk walk should be enough for your Lhasa Apso's exercise needs. While you can walk around your home daily, taking a break from the usual and heading to a park or other area can still be great for you and your dog. It can be a small escape so that you can leave chores for a bit, and your Lhasa Apso will get some mental stimulation from the different location. Take a stroll at a different park once or twice a week, and you will both feel a lot better for the dedicated exercise and escape time.

If your Lhasa Apso is not getting enough activity, it's probably going to be obvious. When a small dog is left to his own devices and has intelligence, it can result in some very undesirable behavior. They aren't known for digging, but if that is an option and a Lhasa Apso is bored, you may find that the dog has dug under a fence or torn up the carpet. Before they get to this point, though, Lhasa Apsos tend to let you know they are bored – they will annoy you first because they want to play. Think of it as a warning, just like when they try to let you know they need to go to the bathroom. Don't ignore those signs, and you can prevent a lot of problematic behavior.

If you are willing to stop and play with him when he is bored, your Lhasa Apso will be happier to interact with you when you want his attention too. Take 15 to 20 minutes to entertain your dog with a bit of training or other activity that gets your dog tired.

Photo Courtesy of Caroline Major

You can actually jog with your Lhasa Apso if he is interested. They are not good for long jogs, with 30 minutes being as much as they can usually handle. Of course, it will be a slower jog considering the dog's size, so you will need to take your pacing from your Lhasa Apso. He will also need to be well trained so that he doesn't try to chase animals while you are jogging. You may want to make sure that your Lhasa Apso's hair is cut a bit shorter for jogs.

There will be days when it is rainy, too cold, too hot, or you just don't feel like going outside, and this is where having a Lhasa Apso is amazing – you don't have to leave home to help him get adequate exercise. You have a wealth of fun activities that you and your Lhasa Apso can enjoy from the comfort of your warm home.

Outdoor Activities

Lhasa Apsos can enjoy the outdoors, but a small backyard is enough for them to play in. A weekly trip to a park or somewhere different is welcome, but they don't require it like a lot of other intelligent dogs. Still, most Lhasa Apso will appreciate a chance to get out and play.

Beach Time!

If you want to go to the beach, your Lhasa Apso will almost certainly love a trip with the family and can be incredibly entertaining while you are there. You will need to make sure that the beach allows for dogs. As long as the beach is dog-friendly, you and your Lhasa Apso can enjoy a nice stroll along the sand—it is much easier on paws than concrete or asphalt.

You can play fetch or let your dog enjoy digging on the beach. If you are making sand-castles or want a quick game of Frisbee or keep away, your dog will love to be a part of the games. You can even bury some of his toys and watch your Lhasa Apso enthusiasti-cally retrieve them. It will be easiest if you have plastic toys so that you don't have to spend a lot of time clean-ing sand out of the toys when you return home.

HELPFUL TIP
How Much Exercise is Enough?

Lhasa Apsos require a moderate amount of exercise. Most will be happy with a daily walk lasting around 30 minutes. Playtime also makes up an essential part of your dog's daily exercise needs, either in the backyard or inside with his favor-ite toys or puzzle games.

If your dog's hair is long, you may not want to take him close to the water. Note that Lhasa Apsos are not particularly adept at swimming. It will also be a lot harder for you to properly groom your dog if he has wet hair and a lot of sand tangled in it. Don't take your dog far in the water. If you just stay where your dog can keep his paws on the sand, your Lhasa Apso can be a good bit of entertainment for you and the family.

Homemade Obstacles

If you have a yard, even a small one, you can set up an obstacle course for your Lhasa Apso. A homemade obstacle course can give you both a bit of time outside, tiring out your dog without you having to expend much energy.

- All you need are small orange cones or light plastics to create a weaving obstacle course, and you can train your dog to run around them.

- If you have lightweight, collapsible tunnels, these are perfect for tunnel training. If you don't have them, cardboard boxes can work just as well, and you don't need them to be big to provide a great obstacle course.

- Ramps are easy as well – a few solid planks and cinder blocks are all you need to create a ramp for training. Make sure the ramp is solid and about twice the width of your dog. Don't make them very high off the ground.

If you can create a little maze for your Lhasa Apso, that's even better. Put a treat in the middle of it to really give your dog an incentive.

Great Walking Companion

As long as it isn't too hot or too cold outside, a nice 30-minute walk around the neighborhood once a day is the perfect daily exercise for your dog. Your Lhasa Apso will probably be bouncy and proud or curious and excited as you stroll around the blocks. If there is a nearby park, this will be a great place to go. It isn't likely that your dog will need a frequent change of venue for the walks, making it easier to walk with your pup on a regular basis.

Fetch!

Lhasa Apsos can excel at fetch, making it another way to tire out your little dog without having to tire out yourself. A couple of tennis balls is all you need to keep your Lhasa Apso happily occupied for as long as you want to throw the ball. It may take a while to convince your Lhasa Apso to drop the ball for the fetch part, which is why you may want more than one. Your dog may think that you should be playing keep away, in which case you can play a bit of chase. Whatever game you end up playing, your Lhasa Apso will probably be incredibly pleased.

Photo Courtesy of Ally Colquitt

Dog Parks

Since there are fantastic odds that your Lhasa Apso is going to be sociable (particularly if you socialized him early on), taking time a couple of days a week to head to a dog park will mean other dogs can tire your pupper out. Give him about 30 minutes of playtime, and he'll probably be more than ready to go home. During the summer, plan to go in the early to middle of the morning. Dog parks are a great way to socialize your dog, though you will need to be careful in the early days to make sure your dog enjoys the playtime.

Photo Courtesy of Jane Wenckus

Note that if your dog doesn't seem particularly happy being with other dogs, this may not be the best way to spend time outside the home.

Indoor Activities

Many of the activities that you do outside can be duplicated inside. You probably won't want to encourage running or throwing items inside (make sure to lay down the law to ensure your children don't try to bring these activities inside), but with your dog's small size, you can easily create some great play settings for your Lhasa Apso.

The Indoor Dig

All you have to do is put down pillows, blankets, or towels, and your dog can have his own indoor digging area. Hide a toy or a treat in the middle and watch as your dog throws himself into trying to find what you have hidden.

Photo Courtesy of Deborah Turner

It's easy to set up, and it doesn't take much to hide a toy or another treat again once the first one is located. Your dog does most of the work, and you get to be entertained.

Hide and Seek

Lhasa Apsos can get incredibly excited when you try to hide from them. Provide some kind of distraction or ask a family member to hold your dog, and you can hurry and hide in another room. It isn't going to take long before your dog finds you, but playing a few times will be more than enough to get your dog tired.

Once your dog learns all the basic commands (Chapter 11), you might be able to get your Lhasa Apso to sit and stay until you call for him to come find you.

Dog Fishing

Like fetch, this game doesn't require much energy on your part but can tire your Lhasa Apso pretty quickly. Tie one of his favorite toys to the end of a stick, then drag it around near your dog. You can use an actual fishing rod if you want, but make sure there are no hooks on it. Move the toy over your dog's head, move in circles, or zigzag with it to get your Lhasa Apso's heart racing. Occasionally, your dog will "bite," and you can "reel him in" by bringing the toy toward you.

Be careful not to pull too hard once your dog catches the toy.

Make sure to play this game in an open space so that your dog doesn't get hurt in all the excitement.

What to Avoid

There are a lot of things you can do to exercise a Lhasa Apso, but with an intelligent dog like this, you have to be very careful about not letting him get into trouble. The following are things you should avoid.

Leaving Him Alone Outside

As your Lhasa Apso is a small-sized dog, you may have to worry about him being snatched by a bird of prey, so he needs to be supervised while outside. Also, when it's time for a potty break, always go with your dog as he may find a hole in the fence or even dig one. Yes, putting your dog out in the backyard alone is easier, especially if you are running late for work or it's snowing or raining. But the time you save is negated if your dog manages to get out of your yard because you weren't watching him. Never put your dog outside and hope that he will get his daily exercise. It's an activity that requires both of you—especially since your bored Lhasa Apso will learn that getting out of the yard will get him more attention as you try to chase him.

Off-Leash

Unless you are at a dog park or in a fenced-in location, don't take your Lhasa Apso off the leash. He may start chasing an animal and get lost or hurt. Trying to call out to your Lhasa Apso to get him to stop is not likely to be effective, especially if he isn't responding well to training. For safety's sake, just keep him on the leash.

PART 4
TAKING CARE OF YOUR LHASA APSO

CHAPTER 14
Nutrition

Proper nutrition for a Lhasa Apso is a little different than for many other breeds because of their long-haired coats. To properly care for the coat, they need more protein and a bit more fat, making their diet an interesting balancing act.

It's a good thing that they tend to be picky eaters because some Lhasa Apsos have sensitive stomachs. Selecting hypoallergenic food and being very choosy about what foods you give your dog will definitely help him to live longer and have fewer stomach issues.

Why a Healthy Diet is Important

Just because your Lhasa Apso is active doesn't mean he is burning all the calories he takes in, especially if you have an open treat policy. Just as you should not be eating all day, your puppy shouldn't be either. If you have a busy schedule, it will be too easy for your dog to have substantial lapses in activity levels while you are not ensuring he gets the recommended daily exercise (covered in Chapter 14).

You need to be aware of roughly how many calories your dog eats a day, including treats, so be mindful of your dog's weight and whether or not he is putting on pounds. This will tell you if you should adjust his food intake or if you should change the food to something more nutritious but with fewer calories.

Always talk with your vet if you have concerns about your Lhasa Apso's weight.

Dangerous Foods

Dogs can eat raw meat without having to worry about the kinds of problems a person would encounter. However, there are some human foods that could be fatal to your Lhasa Apso.

The following is a list of foods you should **NEVER** feed your dog:

- Apple seeds
- Chocolate
- Coffee
- Cooked bones (They can kill a dog when the bones splinter in the dog's mouth or stomach.)
- Corn on the cob (The cob is deadly to dogs; corn off the cob is fine.)
- Grapes/raisins
- Macadamia nuts
- Onions and chives
- Peaches, persimmons, and plums
- Tobacco (Your Lhasa Apso will not realize it is not a food and may eat it if it's left out.)
- Xylitol (a sugar substitute in candies and baked goods)
- Yeast

In addition to this list, consult the Canine Journal for a lengthy list of other dangerous foods. (http://www.caninejournal.com/foods-not-to-feed-dog/)

Canine Nutrition

Canines are largely carnivorous, and protein is a significant dietary need. However, they need more than just protein to be healthy.

The following table provides the primary nutritional require-ments for dogs:

Nutrient	Sources	Puppy	Adult
Protein	meat, eggs, soybeans, corn, wheat, peanut butter	22.0% of diet	18.0% of diet
Fats	fish oil, flaxseed oil, canola oil, pork fat, poultry fat, safflower oil, sunflower oil, soybean oil	8.0 to 15.0% of diet	5.0 to 15.0% of diet
Calcium	dairy, animal organ tissue, meats, legumes (typically beans)	1.0% of diet	0.6% of diet
Phosphorus	meat and pet supplements	0.8% of diet	0.5% of diet
Sodium	meat, eggs	0.3% of diet	0.06% of diet

The following are the remaining nutrients dogs require, all of them less than 1% of a puppy or an adult diet:

- Arginine
- Histidine
- Isoleucine
- Leucine
- Lysine
- Methionine + cystine
- Threonine
- Tryptophan
- Valine
- Chloride

It is best to avoid giving your dog human foods with a lot of sodium and preservatives. Water is also absolutely essential to keep your dog healthy. There should always be water in your dog's water bowl, so make a habit of checking it several times a day so that your dog does not get dehydrated.

HELPFUL TIP
Food Storage

A bag of dog food is a tempting treat for more than just your dog. Mice and other rodents may be encouraged to take up residence in your home or garage if bags of pet food are left out instead of being properly sealed. To deter pests and keep your dog's food fresh, consider purchasing a plastic, metal, or ceramic sealable container for dog food storage.

Proteins and Amino Acids

Since dogs are carnivores, protein is one of the most important nutrients in a healthy dog's diet. (Dogs should not eat as much meat as their close wolf relatives do. Dogs' diets and needs have changed significantly since they have become human companions.) Proteins contain the necessary amino acids for your dog to produce glucose, which is essential for giving your dog energy. A lack of protein in your dog's diet will result in him being lethargic. His coat may start to look dull, and he is likely to lose weight. Conversely, if your dog gets too much protein, his body will store the excess protein as fat, and he will gain weight.

Meat is the best source of protein for your dog, and a dog's dietary needs are significantly different from a human's needs. If you plan to feed your dog a vegetarian diet, it is very important that you talk to your vet first. It is incredibly difficult to ensure that a carnivore receives adequate protein while on a vegetarian diet. Puppies, in particular, need to have adequate protein to be healthy adults, so you may need to give your puppy a diet with meat, then switch to a vegetarian diet after your Lhasa Apso becomes an adult.

Protein is particularly important for taking care of your Lhasa Apso's coat. While you don't want to be excessive, do make sure that your dog gets adequate protein every day. This will be easier if you make meals for your dog. If you don't have time, make sure to buy foods that are high in protein.

Fat and Fatty Acids

Most fats that your dog needs are found in meat. Seed oils provide a lot of necessary healthy fats, too, with peanut butter being one of the most common sources. Fats break down into fatty acids, which your dog needs for fat-soluble vitamins that help with regular cell functions. Perhaps the most obvious benefit of fats and fatty acids can be seen in your dog's coat. Your dog's coat will look and feel much healthier when your dog is getting the right nutrients.

The following is a list of potential health issues that might arise if your dog does not get adequate fats in his daily diet:

- His coat will look less healthy.
- His skin may be dry and itchy.
- His immune system could be compromised, making it easier for your dog to get sick.
- He may have an increased risk of heart disease. The primary concern if your dog gets too much fat is that he will become obese, leading to additional health problems.

Carbohydrates and Cooked Foods

Dogs have been living with humans for millennia, so their dietary needs have evolved like our own. They can eat foods with carbohydrates to supplement the energy typically provided by proteins and fats. If you cook grains (such as barley, corn, and rice) prior to feeding them to your dog, it will be easier for him to digest those complex carbohydrates. If your dog is allergic to grains, potatoes and sweet potatoes are also high in carbohydrates.

Different Dietary Requirements for Different Life Stages

Different stages of a dog's life have different nutritional needs.

Puppy Food

During roughly the first 12 months of their lives, puppies' bodies are growing. To be healthy, they need more calories and have different nutritional needs to promote growth, so feed them a food made specifically for puppies. Puppies can have up to four meals a day. Just be careful not to overfeed them, particularly if you use treats during training. Their nutritional needs are much different from their adult counterparts.

Adult Dog Food

The primary difference between puppy food and adult dog food is puppy food is higher in calories and nutrients, which promote growth. Dog food manufacturers reduce these nutrients in adult dog food, as they no longer need lots of calories to sustain growth. As a rule, when a canine reaches about 90% of his predicted adult size, you should switch to adult dog food.

The size of your Lhasa Apso is key in determining how much to feed him. The following table is a general recommendation for daily food consumption for your adult Lhasa Apso. Initially, you may want to focus on the calories as you try to find the right balance for your dog.

Dog Size	Calories per day
10 lbs.	420 during hot months 630 during cold months
20 lbs.	700 during hot months 1,050 during cold months

You can feed your Lhasa Apso two or three times a day, so you can divide up the calories according to this schedule. Keep in mind these recommendations are per day and not per meal. To make sure your dog feels like a real part of the family, let your pup eat when you do, even if he doesn't get that much food at a time.

If you plan to add wet food, pay attention to the total calorie intake, and adjust how much you feed your dog between the kibble and wet food. The total calories in the kibble and wet food should balance out so as not to exceed your dog's needs. The same is true if you give your dog a lot of treats over the course of the day. You should factor treat calories into how much you feed your dog at mealtimes.

If you feed your dog homemade food (discussed later in this chapter), you should learn your nutrition facts, and you should pay close attention to calories instead of cup measurements.

Senior Dog Food

Senior dogs are not always capable of being as active as they were in their younger days. If you notice your dog is slowing down or suffers joint pain and shows a lack of stamina when taking long walks, you can assume your Lhasa Apso is entering his senior years. Consult with your vet if you think it is time to change the type of food you feed your dog.

The primary difference between adult and senior dog food is senior dog food contains less fat and more antioxidants to help fight weight gain.

Senior dogs also need more protein, which will probably make your dog happy because that usually means more meat. Protein helps to maintain your dog's aging muscles. He should also be eating less phosphorus during his golden years to avoid the risk of developing hyperphosphatemia. This is a condition where dogs have excessive amounts of phosphorus in their bloodstream, and older dogs are at greater risk of developing it. The level of phosphorus in the body is controlled by the kidneys; as such, elevated levels of phosphorus are usually an indication of a problem with the kidneys.

Photo Courtesy of Kirsty Hambleton

Senior dog food has the correct number of calories for reduced activity, which means no adjustment of quantity is needed unless you notice weight gain. Consult your vet if you notice your dog is putting on weight because this could be a sign of illness.

Your Dog's Meal Options

You have three primary choices for what to feed your dog, or you can use a combination of the three, depending on your situation and your dog's specific needs.

Commercial Food

Make sure that you are buying the best dog food you can afford. Take the time to research each of your options, particularly the nutritional value of the food, and review this annually. Make sure the food you are giving your dog is high quality, and always take into account your dog's size, energy level, and age. Your puppy may not need puppy food for as long as other breeds, and dog food for seniors may not be necessary for Lhasa Apsos. You'll need

*Photo Courtesy
of Izabela Sokolowska-Nowak*

to pay attention to your dog's individual needs to determine if he needs a special food for his age.

The website Pawster provides several great articles about which commercial dog foods are best for Lhasa Apsos. Since new foods frequently come on the market, check periodically to see if there are new, better foods that have become available.

If you aren't sure which brand of food is best, talk with the breeder about the foods they recommend. Breeders are really the best guides for you here, as they are experts, but you can also ask your vet.

Some dogs may be picky eaters that get tired of repeatedly eating the same food. While you shouldn't frequently change the brand of food because that can upset your dog's stomach, you can get foods that have assorted flavors. You can also change the taste by adding a bit of wet (canned) food. Adding one-fourth to one-third of a can for each meal is an easy change to make to ensure your dog's happiness.

For more details on commercial options, check out the website Dog Food Advisor. They provide reviews on various dog food brands, as well as providing information on recalls and contamination issues.

COMMERCIAL DRY FOOD

Dry dog food often comes in bags, and it is what the vast majority of people feed their dogs.

PROS OF DRY DOG FOOD:	CONS OF DRY DOG FOOD:
Convenience	Requires research to ensure you don't buy doggie junk food
Variety	Packaging is not always honest
Availability	Recalls for food contamination
Affordability	Loose FDA nutritional regulations
Manufacturers follow nutritional recommendations. (Not all of them follow this, so do your brand research before you buy.)	Low-quality food may have questionable ingredients
Specially formulated for different canine life-stages	
Can be used for training	
Easy to store	

The convenience and ease on your budget mean you are almost certainly going to buy kibble for your dog. This is perfectly fine, and most dogs will be more than happy to eat kibble. Be sure you know what brand you are feeding your dog, and pay attention to kibble recalls so you can stop feeding your dog a certain brand if necessary. Check out the following sites regularly for recall information:

- Dog Food Recalls – www.dogfoodadvisor.com
- American Kennel Club – www.AKC.org
- Dog Food Guide – www.dogfood.guide

COMMERCIAL WET FOOD

Most dogs prefer wet dog food over kibble, but it is also more expensive. Wet dog food can be purchased in large packs that can be extremely easy to store.

PROS OF WET DOG FOOD:	CONS OF WET DOG FOOD:
Helps keep dogs hydrated	Dog bowls must be washed after every meal
Has a richer scent and flavor	Can soften bowel movements
Easier to eat for dogs with dental problems (particularly those with missing teeth) or if a dog has been ill	Can be messier than kibble
Convenient and easy to serve	Once opened, it has a short shelf-life and should be covered and refrigerated
Unopened, it can last between one and three years	More expensive than dry dog food and comes in small quantities
Balanced based on current pet nutrition recommendations	Packaging is not always honest
	Recalls for food contamination
	Loose FDA regulations

Like dry dog food, wet dog food is convenient, and picky dogs are much more likely to eat it than kibble. If your dog gets sick, use wet dog food to ensure that he is still eating and gets the necessary nutrition each day. It may be harder to switch back to kibble once your Lhasa Apso is healthy, but you can always add a little wet food to make each meal more appetizing.

Raw Diet

For dogs prone to food allergies, raw diets can help prevent an allergic reaction to wheat and processed foods. Raw diets are heavy in raw meats, bones, vegetables, and specific supplements. Some of the benefits of a raw diet include:

- Improves your dog's coat and skin
- Improves immune system
- Improves health (as a result of better digestion)
- Increases energy
- Increases muscle mass

Raw diets are meant to give your dog the kind of food canines ate before being domesticated. It means giving your dog uncooked meats, whole (uncooked) bones, and a small amount of dairy products. It doesn't include processed food of any kind—not even food cooked in your kitchen.

There are potential risks to this diet. Dogs have been domesticated for millennia, and their digestive systems have also evolved. Trying to force them to eat the kind of diet they ate hundreds of years ago does not always work as intended, primarily because they may not be able to fully digest raw food the way their ancestors did.

There are also many risks associated with feeding dogs uncooked meals, particularly if the food has been contaminated. Things like bacteria pose a serious risk and can be transferred to you if your dog gets sick. Many medical professionals also warn about the dangers of giving dogs bones even if they are uncooked. Bones can splinter in your dog's mouth and puncture the esophagus or stomach.

The *Canine Journal* (www.caninejournal. com) provides a lot of

Photo Courtesy of Tracy Kiely

information about a raw diet, including different recipes and how to transition your dog to this diet. Always talk to your veterinarian before putting your dog on a new kind of diet.

Homemade Diet

The best home-cooked meals should be planned in advance so that your Lhasa Apso gets the correct nutritional balance. Typically, 50 percent of your dog's food should be animal protein (fish, poultry, and organ meats). About 25 percent should be full of complex carbohydrates. The remaining 25 percent should be from fruits and vegetables, particularly foods like pumpkin, apples, bananas, and green beans. These foods provide extra flavor your Lhasa Apso will probably love while filling him up faster and reducing the chance of overeating.

The following are a few sites where you can learn how to make homemade meals for canines. Most of them are not breed-specific, so if you have more than one dog, these meals can be made for all your furry canine friends:

- Homemade Baked Dry Dog Food for a Lhasa Apso (https://www.petcarerx.com/article/homemade-baked-dry-dog-food-for-a-lhasa-apso/476)
- Easy Homemade Dog Food Recipe (https://thismessisours.com/easy-homemade-dog-food-recipe/)
- Tasty Low Carb (https://www.tasty-lowcarb.com/healthy-homemade-dog-food/)
- Hublore (http://hublore.blogspot.com/2011/05/homemade-dog-food-recipe.html)
- Homemade Dog Food with a Special Ingredient (https://pethelpful.com/dogs/Homemade-Dog-Food-with-an-Extra-Special-Ingredient)
- Canine Journal (https://www.caninejournal.com/homemade-dog-food-recipes/)
- DIY Homemade Dog Food (https://damndelicious.net/2015/04/27/diy-homemade-dog-food/)

Keep in mind the foods your Lhasa Apso absolutely should not eat. You can also mix some of the food you make for yourself into your Lhasa Apso's meal. Do not feed your Lhasa Apso from your plate! Split the food, placing your dog's meal into a bowl so that your canine understands your food is just for you.

Scheduling Meals

> *Feed measured amounts of quality food on a regular schedule. Baby puppies should eat three times daily. After six months and thru adulthood, two meals a day are appropriate. Avoid filling the bowl without measuring as this will often create either a finicky eater (because they overeat at one meal, they are not interested in eating the next) or an obese dog.*
>
> KATHLEEN WALCOTT
> *Floral Hill Lhasa Apsos*

Your Lhasa Apso will probably expect you to stick to a schedule, which definitely includes mealtimes. If treats and snacks are something you establish as a normal routine, your dog will expect that too! For puppies, plan to have three or four meals, while adults and seniors should typically have two meals a day.

Food Allergies and Intolerance

Whenever you start your dog on a new type of food (even if it's simply a different flavor), you need to monitor him while he becomes accustomed to the change. Food allergies are fairly common in Lhasa Apsos, and the symptoms manifest themselves as hot spots, which are similar to rashes in humans. Your dog may start scratching or chewing specific spots on his body, and his fur or hair could start falling out around those spots. Some dogs don't have individual hot spots, but the allergy shows up on their entire coat. If your Lhasa Apso seems to be shedding more hair than normal, take him to the vet to be checked for food allergies.

If you give your dog something his stomach cannot handle, it will probably be obvious when your dog is unable to hold his bowels. If he is already house-trained, he will probably either pant at you or whimper to let you know he needs to go outside. Get him outside as quickly as you can so that he does not have an accident. Flatulence will also probably occur more often if your Lhasa Apso has a food intolerance.

Since the symptoms of food allergies and intolerances look similar to a reaction to nutritional deficiencies, you should visit your vet immediately! This is especially true if you notice any problems with your dog's coat or skin.

CHAPTER 15

Grooming – Productive Bonding

> "
>
> *If you get a puppy, get it used to being brushed and having things around the face. A groomer's worst nightmare is grooming a Lhasa's face while it is trying to eat your finger. Use a capped pen and run it all along the face and below the eyes. This will simulate a groomer's scissors when the time comes. Do this for two minutes at a time with the brush and pen. Always remember to make training fun or relaxing*
>
> CHOO MICHAEL YANG
> *Yangchoo Lhasa Apso*
>
> "

Those long, luxurious coats are much easier to groom than you may think, but they can also cause problems, including skin conditions (Chapter 17). By grooming him every day, you can make sure to take care of his skin and keep it from getting irritated and keep the hair from getting tangled and matted. It also means that you need to be careful when you brush him so that you don't hurt him.

Grooming Tools

When it comes to their coats, Lhasa Apsos are both easy and difficult to groom. If you don't take care of it daily (or nearly every day), it can cause problems. You won't need too many tools to properly tend to your dog's coat—the biggest investment will be in time. The following are the recommended tools to best tend to your dog's coat:

- A slicker brush or a two-sided pin/bristle brush—this will help you to remove the tangles without hurting your dog.
- A steel comb
- A fulminator to remove extra hair from the undercoat or an undercoat rake
- Besides the brush, you will need to get a few other tools to properly take care of your pup.
- Shampoo (Make sure you use dog shampoo, not human, and check Bark Space for the latest recommendations.)
- Nail trimmers
- Toothbrush and dog toothpaste (not human—it's toxic for dogs!) (Check the American Kennel Club for the latest recommendations for the Lhasa Apso, as they tend to have dental problems.)

Coat Management

> "
>
> *The best thing you can do for you both is to teach the dog to lay on its side and brush them. This allows you to get underneath where the worst matting happens, like under the arms. If the dog is trained to lie on its side, it is relaxing for everyone with no fighting the grooming session. Control is the key. Trying to get matts out of dog that will only stand or 'hunker down' on its stomach for grooming makes a stressful situation for the dog and the groomer whether it is the owner or pro groomer. It also can set up for biting when the dog's matts are hard to get to. This is a coated breed and no matter how short you keep it cut matts are inevitable.*
>
> CARLA VARNEY
> *Hi Tide Lhasa Apsos*
>
> "

Always make sure to tire your dog before you start brushing. You cannot rush the process. To get all of the tangles and other issues taken care of, you are going to need a good bit of time, so you need your dog to sit still for a while. You'll know when you don't need to dedicate time to tiring your dog when he starts to slow down as a senior or shows an interest in just sitting and letting you pet and brush him.

HELPFUL TIP
Detangling Your Lhasa Apso

The Lhasa Apso's distinctive coat is one of the breed's most charming features, but these luscious locks can become tangled and matted without frequent brushing. Using a detangler or leave-in conditioner as part of your dog's daily grooming maintenance can help stop tangles in their tracks. If knots happen, work through them with a metal comb after teasing them apart gently with your fingers as much as possible. Do not wet your Lhasa Apso's fur before attempting to remove a knot. Wet hair is more difficult to untangle and more brittle than dry hair.

Puppies

The difficulty when grooming a puppy is fairly universal because puppies are notorious for squirming! A daily brushing is the best way to both reduce how much your puppy sheds and to bond with your dog. Yes, it will be a bit challenging in the beginning because puppies don't sit still for prolonged periods of time; there will be a lot of wiggling and attempts to play. Trying to tell your puppy that the brush is not a toy clearly won't work, so be patient during each brushing session!

On the other hand, your pup will be so adorable that you probably won't mind a grooming session taking a bit longer than expected. Just make sure you let your pup know grooming is serious business, and playing comes after grooming. Otherwise, your Lhasa Apso is always going to try to play, which will make brushing him more time-consuming.

Try planning to brush your puppy after a vigorous exercise session. If you find your puppy has trouble sitting still, you can make brushing sessions shorter, but do it more than once a day until he gets used to the routine.

Adult Dogs

Brushing needs to be done daily for the adults, especially after a lot of outdoor activity. Whatever brush you find works for your dog, the brushings should be both relaxing to your pup and beneficial for his skin. The grooming process stimulates the skin to release oils that make the fur shinier and more resistant to dirt, and this is absolutely necessary for Lhasa Apsos. If you regularly brush your dog, it can help reduce how often you have to bathe your Lhasa Apso.

Brushing your dog is about more than just removing excess fur and improving the coat's shine. You need to spend each grooming session looking for skin problems, lumps, flea or tick bites, and other problems when you brush your buddy. Brushing reveals potential issues that you should monitor, and if symptoms become severe, you should have them checked out at the vet's office.

If you rescued an adult Lhasa Apso, it might take a little while to get the dog used to being brushed frequently. If your dog does not feel comfortable in the beginning when you brush his fur, work the routine into your schedule, just like training, so he will get accustomed to the task.

Senior Dogs

You can brush your senior dog more often if you would like, as the extra affection and time you give him will probably be welcome. After all, he's slowing down, and just relaxing with you will be enjoyable for him (and the warmth of your hands will feel really good on his aging body). Grooming sessions are an appropriate time to check for problems while giving your older pup a nice massage to ease any pain. Look for any changes to the skin, such as bumps or fatty lumps. These may need to be mentioned to the vet during a regular visit.

Allergies

Some Lhasa Apsos have skin allergies. If your Lhasa Apso is suffering from hot spots, or if you notice his coat is thinning, then you should look for the following allergic reactions:

- Wounds take longer to heal
- Weak immune system
- Aching joints
- Hair is falling out
- Ear infections

Regular brushing keeps you aware of the health of your Lhasa Apso's coat. This will help you identify when your little dear is suffering from allergies so that you can take him to the vet immediately.

Bath Time

Since regular brushing helps stimulate the natural oils of the breed, most Lhasa Apso people recommend just bathing as needed. If you prefer to be able to set a schedule, once a quarter (once every three months) or twice a year will probably keep your Lhasa Apso from getting stinky. If your Lhasa Apso gets muddy or really dirty, make sure to bathe him so that the dirt and mud don't get trapped in his hair. Avoid bathing him too often, though, since it can irritate your dog's skin and remove necessary oils in his hair.

Photo Courtesy of Izabela Sokolowska-Nowak

Whenever you go exploring or hiking with your Lhasa Apso, most likely, you will need to bathe your canine after each adventure. Make sure the water isn't too cold or too hot but comfortably warm, and always avoid getting his head wet. How to wash your dog's face is covered in the next section.

1. Gather everything you will need before you start your dog's bath. At a minimum, you need the following:

A shampoo and conditioners made specifically for dogs

B cup for pouring water (if bathing in a tub)

C towels

D brushes for after the drying process

E nonslip tub mat if you use a tub

F buckets and a hose to rinse off if you bathe your dog outside

2. Take your Lhasa Apso out for a walk. This will tire your dog and make him a little hotter and less fearful—he might even appreciate the bath's cooling effect.

3. Run the water, making sure the temperature is lukewarm but not hot, especially if you have just finished a walk. If you are washing your Lhasa Apso in a bathtub, you only need enough water to cover your pup's stomach. Do not fully cover your dog's body.

4. Pick up your dog if you are using a bathtub, and talk in a strong, confident voice.

5. Place the dog in the tub and use the cup to wash the dog. Don't use too much soap—it isn't necessary. You can fully soak the dog, starting at the neck and going to the rump. It is fine to get him wet and to suds him up all at once, or you can do it a little at a time if your dog is very wiggly. Just make sure you don't get any water on his head.

6. Confidently talk to your Lhasa Apso while you are bathing him.

Photo Courtesy of Judith Coulson

7. Make sure you don't pour water on your dog's head or in his eyes or ears. Use a wet hand and gently scrub. (Follow the steps in the next section for how to carefully wash your dog's face and ears.)

8. When you rinse, make sure to brush up against the fur so that there is no shampoo left.

Photo Courtesy
of Katherine Miller

9. Take your Lhasa Apso out of the water and towel him dry.

10. Make sure to give special attention to drying around the head and face.

11. Brush your dog when you are finished.

12. Give him a treat if he was particularly upset about the bath.

You can use these practices with other kinds of bathing, such as outside or at a public washing facility; modify them as necessary.

The first few times you bathe your dog, pay attention to the things that bother or scare him. If he is afraid of running water, make sure you don't have the water running when your dog is in the tub. If he moves around a lot when you start to apply the shampoo, it could indicate the smell is too strong. Modify the process as necessary in order to make it as comfortable for your dog as possible.

Keep a calm, loving tone as you wash your dog to make the process a little easier next time. Sure, your Lhasa Apso may whine, throw a tantrum, or wiggle excessively, but a calm reaction will teach your dog that bathing is a necessary part of being a member of the pack.

HELPFUL TIP
Bonding over Brushing

Bringing home a new puppy can be overwhelming, especially when deciding what to buy. Since Lhasa Apsos will need frequent grooming throughout their life, you can get your grooming relationship off to a great start by introducing brushing as a form of bonding in the first few weeks. Using a soft-bristled slicker brush or rubber brush, let your puppy sniff the new brush before working in small segments with the brush. Having a handful of small treats ready can help your dog associate brushing with the positive experience of receiving a treat!

Cleaning Eyes and Ears

When bathing your dog, use a washcloth to wash his face and ears, and ALWAYS avoid getting water in his ears, which can lead to problems.

You will need to make weekly checks around your Lhasa Apso's eyes and ears to detect infections early. The following are signs of a problem:

- Frequent head shaking or tilting
- Regular scratching at ears
- Swollen or red ears

- A smell or discharge from the ears

If you notice any problems with your Lhasa Apso's ears, make an appointment with your vet. Never try to treat an infection on your own; hydrogen peroxide, cotton swabs, and other cleaning tools should never be used in a dog's ears. Your vet can show you how to clean your dog's ears correctly.

Lhasa Apsos have a few genetic eye and ear conditions (See Chapter 17), so take time to always check your dog's eyes while you are grooming him.

Cataracts are a fairly common problem for all dogs as they age. If you see cloudy eyes, have your Lhasa Apso checked.

Trimming Nails

Cutting a Lhasa Apso's nails can be difficult because dogs can be sensitive about someone touching their paws. Odds are your dog will have dark nails, which makes it difficult to cut them to the correct length without accidentally cutting the quick, the most sensitive part of the nail. It's best to have an expert cut your dog's nails until you understand how nail trimming is done. If you have never cut a dog's nails, ask a professional, like a groomer or a vet, to teach you the steps involved because nails can bleed a lot if they are not cut properly. If you know how to trim a dog's nails, make sure to have some styptic powder nearby in case you cut the nail too close.

If you want to trim your dog's nails yourself, there are nail grinders that can help lessen your worry about cutting the quick, but you will need to make sure you don't grind too much off the nail. Seek help from a professional before using the grinder, keep your dog calm during the process, and always think of your dog's safety first.

To know when your pup needs his nails cut, listen for clicking sounds on hard surfaces when your dog is walking. Those sounds indicate you should trim your dog's nails on a more frequent basis. As a general rule, once a month is recommended.

Photo Courtesy of Helen and Sam Linklater

Dogs' nails have a small vein that runs through them, and for dogs with white nails, you can see the pink vein. If your dog has black nails, never try to cut his nails without getting professional assistance a few times first because you cannot see where that vein ends, and you will need to learn to avoid cutting the nail too much.

Once you are comfortable cutting your dog's nails, you will need a set of nail clippers for small- to medium-sized dog paws (depending on the size of your Lhasa Apso).

1. Take your dog's paw gently and firmly. If your dog squirms, you may need to tire out your dog before trying to cut his nails.

2. Push any hair away from the nail you want to cut.

3. Look for the pink vein (if your dog has light-colored nails), then be mindful of it as you prepare to cut the first nail.

4. Position the nail clipper where the nail begins to curve, making sure the vein is not going to be cut.

5. Check the under part of the nail to see if you can see a pinkish-gray area. If you can see it, do not cut any further. If you don't see it and you want to cut a little more, repeat step four.

You will need to repeat this process for every nail on all four paws.

* If your dog's nail starts to bleed, apply styptic powder or silver nitrate sticks (the sticks are less messy) to the area. Follow the directions on the container to help stem the flow. Continue to hold your dog's paw until it stops bleeding before you let go of your dog. You can use hydrogen peroxide to clean up the blood on the fur after the nail stops bleeding.

If you only cut a little each time, you will need to cut your dog's nails once a month. If you cut a little further, you may be able to cut his nails just once a quarter.

Oral Health

Since Lhasa Apsos tend to have dental issues, it is best to be extra careful with your Lhasa Apso's oral hygiene. Besides healthy food, there are two recommendations to take care of your Lhasa Apso's teeth.

1. Brush your Lhasa Apso's teeth twice a week.

2. Give your Lhasa Apso dental chew treats.

Brushing Your Dog's Teeth

You have to learn to be patient and keep teeth cleaning from being an all-out fight with your dog. Brushing a dog's teeth is a little weird, and your Lhasa Apso may not be terribly happy with someone putting stuff in his mouth. However, once he is accustomed to it, the task will probably only take a few minutes a day. Regular brushing keeps down plaque and tartar, making your pup's teeth healthier.

Always use a toothpaste that is made for dogs; human toothpaste can be toxic for your little friend. There are assorted flavors of dog toothpaste, which will make it easier when brushing your Lhasa Apso's teeth, and it could also be entertaining as he tries to eat the meat-flavored toothpaste!

1. The following are the steps for brushing your dog's teeth:

2. Put a little toothpaste on your finger and hold it out to your dog.

3. Let your dog lick the toothpaste from your finger.

4. Praise your dog for trying something new.

Put a little toothpaste on your finger again, lift your dog's upper lip, and begin to rub in circles along your Lhasa Apso's gums. Your pup will probably make it difficult by constantly trying to lick your finger. Give your puppy praise when he doesn't lick the toothpaste or doesn't wiggle too much.

 Ⓐ Try to move your finger in a circular motion. This will be very tricky, especially if you have a puppy with sharp baby teeth.

 Ⓑ Try to keep the dog still without putting him in a vise. As your puppy gets bigger, he'll need to know how to sit for the cleaning process voluntarily.

5. Try to massage both the top and bottom gums. It is likely the first few times you won't be able to do much more than get your finger in your dog's mouth, and that's okay. Over time, your dog will learn to listen because general behavioral training will reinforce listening to your commands.

6. Stay positive. No, you probably won't be able to clean your dog's teeth properly for a while, and that is perfectly fine—as long as you keep working at it patiently and consistently.

Once your dog seems comfortable having his teeth brushed with your finger, try the same steps with a canine toothbrush. (It could take a couple of weeks before you can graduate to this stage.)

Dental Chews

One of the healthiest treats to give any dog is dental chews. While you will need to keep count of the treats as a part of your dog's daily caloric intake, they help with taking care of your dog's teeth. They aren't a replacement for regular brushing, but they are a good complement. Dogs tend to love these treats, and they help improve your dog's breath, so it is a win-win. Make sure to do your research to ensure that you are giving your dog the healthiest dental chews. You don't want to give your Lhasa Apso any treats that have questionable or uncertain ingredients.

CHAPTER 16

General Health Issues: Allergies, Parasites, and Vaccinations

Lhasa Apsos don't need much time outside, making them at far less risk of a lot of parasites compared to a lot of breeds. That doesn't mean there are no risks—fleas and mosquitoes are both going to love your dog. That long hair isn't much protection against either of these two parasites, so you need to make sure to take all of the necessary precautions to protect your pup. You can also take your Lhasa Apso for short hikes, and that could mean exposure to ticks and other parasites. It is best to be aware of these threats, even if your Lhasa Apso is perfectly happy to play inside most of the time.

Fleas are a universal problem for all dogs because fleas can live in any grass, whether short or long. If you notice rashes or skin irritation, it could be an allergic reaction or symptoms of a parasite. Talk to your vet about all potential environmental risks and any skin conditions you notice when you groom your dog.

The Role of Your Veterinarian

Scheduled veterinary visits, routine vaccinations, and regular checkups make for a healthy Lhasa Apso. If your dog seems sluggish or less excited than usual, it could be a sign there is something wrong with him. Fortunately, the breed's personality tends to make it easy to tell when your dog isn't feeling well. Annual visits to the vet will help catch any problems that might be slowly draining the energy or the health from your dog.

Regular checkups also ensure that your Lhasa Apso is aging well. If your dog shows symptoms of a potential problem, an early diagnosis will address the problem. You and your vet can create a plan to manage any pain or

Photo Courtesy
of Maria Tinham

problems that come with your dog's aging process. The vet may recommend adjustments to your schedule to accommodate your pup's aging body and his diminishing abilities. This will ensure that you can keep having fun together without hurting your dog.

Vets can provide treatment or preventive medication for parasites and other microscopic threats that your dog might encounter on a daily basis, whether playing outside or when he is exposed to dogs or other animals.

Allergies

Dog allergies are usually a result of allergens (such as dust, mold, or pollen), which irritate the skin or nasal passages. Dogs often develop allergies when they are between one and five years old. Once they develop an allergy, canines never outgrow the problem.

The scientific name for environmental allergies is atopic dermatitis. However, it is difficult to know if the problem is environmental or if it is a food you are feeding your dog.

The following symptoms can be seen when either type of allergy is present:

- Itching/scratching, particularly around the face
- Hot spots
- Ear infections
- Skin infections
- Runny eyes and nose (not as common)

Since the symptoms are the same for food and environmental allergies, your vet will help determine the cause. If your dog has a food allergy, change the food that you give him. If he has an environmental allergy, he will need medication, just as humans do. There are several types of medications that can help your dog become less sensitive to allergens:

- Antibacterial/Antifungal – These treatments only address the problems that come with allergies; shampoos, pills, and creams usually do not directly treat the allergy itself.

- Anti-inflammatories – These are over-the-counter medications, which are comparable to allergy medicine for people. Don't give your dog any medication without first consulting with the vet. You will need to monitor your dog to see if he has any adverse effects. If your dog is lethargic, has diarrhea, or shows signs of dehydration, consult with your vet immediately.

- Immunotherapy – This is a series of shots that can help reduce your dog's sensitivity to whatever he is allergic to. You can learn from your vet how to give your dog these shots at home. Scientists are also developing

an oral version of this medication to make it easier to take care of your dog.

- Topical – This medication tends to be a type of shampoo and conditioner that will remove any allergens from your dog's fur. Giving your dog a warm (not hot) bath can also help relieve itching.

To determine the best treatment for your situation, talk with your vet.

HELPFUL TIP
Motion Sickness

If your dog frequently becomes sick when riding in a car, he may be prone to motion sickness. Most dogs outgrow motion sickness by the time they are one year old, but if this problem persists, you may want to talk to your vet about a solution. In many dogs, vomiting can also be caused by anxiety. Be sure to acclimate your dog to car travel before taking long trips.

Inhalant and Environmental Allergies

Inhalant allergies are caused by things like dust, pollen, mold, and dog dander. Your dog might scratch at a particular hotspot, or he might paw at his eyes and ears. Some dogs have runny noses and sneeze prolifically, in addition to scratching.

Contact Allergies

Contact allergies mean that your dog has touched something that triggers an allergic reaction. Things like wool, chemicals in a flea treatment, and certain grasses can trigger irritation in a dog's skin, even causing discoloration. If left untreated, the allergic reaction can cause the affected area to emit a strong odor or cause fur loss.

Like food allergies, contact allergies are easy to treat because once you know what is irritating your dog's skin, you can remove the problem.

Fleas and Ticks

Make it a habit to check for ticks after every outing into the woods or near long grass or wild plants. Comb through your dog's fur and check his skin for signs of irritation and for any parasites. Since you will be doing this several times a week, you should be able to recognize when there's a change, such as a new bump.

Fleas are problematic because they're far more mobile than ticks. The best way to look for fleas is to make it a regular part of your brushing sessions. If you see black specks on the flea comb after brushing through your dog's fur, this could be a sign of fleas.

Instead of using a comb, you can also put your dog on a white towel and run your hand over the fur. Fleas and flea dirt are likely to fall onto the towel. Fleas often are seen on the stomach, so you may notice them when your pup wants a belly rub. You can also look for behavioral indicators, such as incessant scratching and licking. If fleas are a problem, you will need to use flea preventative products on a regular basis once your puppy has reached the appropriate age.

Both fleas and ticks can carry parasites and illnesses that can be passed on to you and your family. Ticks carry Lyme disease, which can be debilitating or deadly if untreated. Lyme disease symptoms include headaches, fever, and fatigue. The bite itself often has a red circle around it. Ticks will fall off your dog once they are full, so if you find a tick on your dog, it will either be looking for a place to latch onto your dog, or it will be feeding. Use the following steps to remove the tick if it has latched onto your dog.

Photo Courtesy of Janita Nixon

- Apply rubbing alcohol to the area where the tick is located.
- Use tweezers to pull the tick off your dog. Do not use your fingers because infections are transmitted through blood, and you don't want the tick to latch onto you.
- Place the tick in a bag and make sure it is secure so that it does not fall out. The vet can assess the type of tick for diagnostic purposes since different types of ticks carry different diseases.
- Examine the spot where the tick was to make sure it is fully removed. Sometimes the head will remain under the dog's skin, so make sure all of the tick has been removed.
- Set up a meeting with the vet to have your dog checked.

The FDA has issued a warning about some store-bought treatments for fleas and ticks. Treatments can be applied monthly, or you can purchase a collar for constant protection. Either way, make sure the treatment does not contain isoxazoline, which can have a negative effect on some pets, such as cats. (This chemical is found in Bravecto, Nexgard, Credelio, and Simparica.)

Most ingredients in these treatments are safe if the proper dose is used. However, if you use a product that is meant for a larger dog, the effects can be toxic to your smaller dog. Consult your vet for recommended treatments and administer the appropriate dose of flea and tick repellant for your dog's size and needs. When you start applying the treatment, watch your dog for the following issues:

- Diarrhea/vomiting
- Trembling
- Lethargy
- Seizures

Take your dog to the vet if you notice any of these issues.

Never use any cat product on a dog and vice versa. If your dog is sick, pregnant, or nursing, you may need to look for an alternative preventative treatment. If you have a cat or young children, you should choose one of the other preventative options for keeping fleas and ticks away. This is because flea collars contain an ingredient that is lethal to felines and that might be carcinogenic to humans.

The packaging on flea treatments will advise you when to begin treating your dog based on his current age and size. Different brands have different recommendations, and you don't want to start treating your puppy too early.

There are also important steps to applying the treatment. Make sure you understand all of the steps before purchasing the flea treatment.

If you want to use natural products instead of chemicals, research the alternatives and decide what works best for your Lhasa Apso. Verify that any natural products work before you buy them, and make sure you consult with your vet. Establish a regular monthly schedule, and add it to your calendar so that you remember to consistently treat your dog for fleas and ticks.

Parasitic Worms

Although worms are a less common problem than fleas and ticks, they can be far more dangerous. The following lists the types of worms that you should be aware of:

- Heartworms
- Hookworms
- Roundworms
- Tapeworms
- Whipworms

Unfortunately, there isn't an easy-to-recognize set of symptoms to help identify when your dog has worms. However, you can keep an eye out for the following symptoms, and if your dog shows any of these warning signs, schedule a visit to the vet:

- Your Lhasa Apso is unexpectedly lethargic for a few days.
- Patches of fur begin to fall out (this will be noticeable if you brush your Lhasa Apso regularly), or you notice patchy spaces in your dog's coat.
- Your dog's stomach becomes distended (expands) and looks like a potbelly.
- Your Lhasa Apso begins coughing, vomiting, has diarrhea, or has a loss of appetite.

If you aren't sure about any symptom, it's always best to get your dog to the vet as soon as possible.

Heartworms

Heartworms are a significant threat to your dog's health and can be deadly, as they can both slow and stop blood flow. As such, you should consistently treat your dog with heartworm protection.

155

Photo Courtesy
of Andrea Dorfner

Fortunately, there are medications that prevent your dog from developing heartworms. To prevent this deadly problem, you can give your dog a chewable medication, topical medicine, or you can request shots.

The heartworm parasite is carried by mosquitoes, which are nearly impossible to avoid in most regions of the country, and it is a condition that is costly and time-consuming to treat. The following are the steps involved in treating your dog for heartworms:

- The vet will draw blood for testing, which can cost as much as $1,000.

- Treatment will begin with some initial medications, including antibiotics and anti-inflammatory drugs.

- Following a month of the initial medication, your vet will give your dog three shots over the course of two months.

From the time of diagnosis until the confirmation your dog is free of heartworms, you will need to be extremely cautious when you exercise your dog because the worms are in your dog's heart, and that inhibits blood flow.

This means raising your dog's heart rate too much could kill him. Your vet will tell you how best to exercise your canine during this time. Considering your Lhasa Apso may be energetic, this could be a very rough time for both you and your dog.

Treatment will continue after the shots are complete. After approximately six months, your vet will conduct another blood test to ensure the worms are gone.

Once your dog is cleared of the parasites, you will need to begin medicating your dog against heartworms in the future. There will be lasting damage to your dog's heart, so you will need to ensure that your dog does not over exercise.

Intestinal Worms: Hookworms, Roundworms, Tapeworms, and Whipworms

All four of these worms thrive in your dog's intestinal tract, and they get there when your dog eats something contaminated. The following are the most common ways dogs ingest worms:

- Feces
- Small hosts, such as fleas, cockroaches, earthworms, and rodents
- Soil, including licking it from their fur and paws
- Contaminated water
- Mother's milk (If the mother has worms, she can pass them on to young puppies when they nurse.)

The following are the most common symptoms and problems caused by intestinal parasites:

- Anemia
- Blood loss
- Coughing
- Dehydration
- Diarrhea
- Large intestine inflammation
- Weight loss
- A pot-bellied appearance

If a dog lies in soil with **hookworm larvae**, the parasites can burrow through the canine's skin. Vets will conduct a diagnostic test to determine if your dog has this parasite, and if your dog does have hookworms, the vet will prescribe a dewormer. If your dog is infested with hookworms, you should visit a doctor yourself because humans can get hookworms, too. Being treated at the same time as your Lhasa Apso will help stop the vicious cycle of continually trading off which of you has worms.

Roundworms are quite common, and at some point in their lives, most dogs have to be treated for them. The parasites primarily eat the digested food in your dog's stomach, getting the nutrients your dog needs. It is possible for larvae to remain in your dog's stomach even after all of the adult worms have been eradicated. If your Lhasa Apso is pregnant, her puppies should be checked periodically to make sure the inactive larvae are not passed on to the puppies. The mother will also need to go through the same testing to make sure the worms don't make her sick.

Tapeworms are usually eaten when they are eggs and are carried by fleas or from the feces of other animals who also have tapeworms. The eggs develop in the canine's small intestine until they reach the adult stage. Over time, parts of the tapeworm will break off and can be seen in your dog's waste. If this happens, you should be very thorough when cleaning up any waste so that other animals will not also contract tapeworms. While tapeworms are not usually fatal, they can cause weight loss and give your dog a potbelly. (The size of your dog's stomach depends on how big the worms grow in your dog's intestines.)

Your vet can test your dog for tapeworms and prescribe medication to take care of the problem. The medication might include chewable tablets, regular tablets, or a powder that can be sprinkled on your dog's food. There is a minimal risk of humans catching tapeworms, but children are at the greatest risk. Be sure children wash their hands carefully when playing in areas used by your dog. It is also possible to contract tapeworms if a person swallows a flea, which is feasible if your dog and home have a serious infestation.

Whipworms grow in the large intestine, and when in large numbers, they can be fatal. Their name is indicative of the appearance of their tails, which are thinner than their upper section. Like the other worms, you will need to have your dog tested to determine if he has acquired whipworms.

Staying current with flea treatments, properly disposing of your pet's waste, and making sure your Lhasa Apso does not eat trash or animal waste will help prevent your dog from getting these parasites.

Medication to prevent these four parasites can often be included in your dog's heartworm medication. Be sure to speak with your vet regarding the different options.

Vaccinating Your Lhasa Apso

Vaccination schedules are routine for most dog breeds, including Lhasa Apsos. Make sure to add this information to your calendar, and until your puppy has completed his vaccinations, he should avoid contact with other dogs.

The following list can help you schedule your Lhasa Apso's vaccinations:

Timeline	Shot		
6 to 8 weeks	Bordetella Lyme	Leptospira Influenza Virus-H3N8	DHPP – First shot Influenza Virus-H3N2
10 to 12 weeks	Leptospira Lyme	DHPP – Second Rabies shot Influenza Virus-H3N8	Influenza Virus-H3N2
14 to 16 weeks	DHPP – Third shot		
Annually	Leptospira Lyme	Bordetella Influenza Virus-H3N8	Rabies Influenza Virus-H3N2
Every 3 Years	DHPP Booster	Rabies (if opted for longer duration vaccination)	

These shots protect your dog against a range of ailments. Keep in mind these shots should be a part of your dog's annual vet visit so that you can continue to keep your pup safe!

Holistic Alternatives

Wanting to prevent exposure to chemical treatments for your dog makes sense, and there are many good reasons why people are moving to more holistic methods. However, if you decide to go with holistic medication, talk with your vet first about reputable options. You can also seek out Lhasa Apso experts for recommendations before you start trying any holistic methods of care.

It is possible something like massage therapy can help your dog, especially as he ages. Even chiropractic therapy is available for dogs, but you will need to be sure to find a reputable chiropractor for your pup, so the treatment doesn't do more harm than good. Follow recommendations on reputable, holistic Lhasa Apso websites to provide the best, safest care for your dog.

CHAPTER 17

Genetic Health Concerns Common to the Lhasa Apso

One of the biggest downsides of Lhasa Apsos is that there are a lot of potential health issues with the breed. A lot of this stems from the length of time the breed has been around and the way that the breeding of dogs has changed over the years—most older breeds have numerous serious issues, so it is not just Lhasa Apsos. Fortunately, most of the common problems are relatively minor, so it is more a matter of watching for problems that reduce the quality of life than ones that pose a serious risk to your Lhasa Apso's life. As the breed has an average lifespan of between 12 and 14 years (though some Lhasa Apsos can live 16 years), you want to make sure you watch for potential problems to help your dog live a long, healthy life.

Photo Courtesy of Betty Umaly

Common Lhasa Apso Health Issues

You want to make sure that you catch health issues early to improve your dog's quality of life. Take the time to monitor your dog for those potential health problems.

Brachycephalic

Lhasa Apsos have longer snouts than the majority of popular brachycephalic breeds, but they are still considered a brachial breed. They won't be nearly so noisy or slobbery as breeds like Bulldogs and Pugs, but Lhasa Apsos can have problems with their airways because of their shorter noses. With their long hair, it is a little more difficult for them to cool down when they get hot. If your Lhasa Apso has trouble breathing, you should avoid more vigorous exercise, especially jogging.

Though you need to be careful about their breathing, Lhasa Apsos have more trouble with their eyes.

Chondrodysplasia

Also called canine dwarfism, chondrodysplasia displays with deformed back and legs. Lhasa Apsos do have very short legs, especially compared to their longer backs. This is one reason it is so important not to pick up your dog. It is much easier to hurt his spine. This disease means Lhasa Apsos are more likely to have orthopedic problems than other dogs.

HEALTH WATCH
Identifying Progressive Retinal Atrophy

Like any breed, Lhasa Apsos are more prone to certain health conditions than others. One of these conditions is progressive retinal atrophy (PRA). There are two versions of this disease, one of which is inherited. Responsible breeders should screen for this genetic condition in their dogs, and dogs who develop PRA should not be used for breeding. One of the earliest signs of PRA is night blindness, which manifests as clumsiness at night or in dark rooms. PRA is not painful but will eventually lead to blindness. Currently, there is no treatment for PRA, but canine blindness is sometimes caused by a different, underlying condition that can be treated. If you notice your dog becoming clumsy or nervous at night, don't hesitate to consult your veterinarian.

Photo Courtesy
of Helen Cloherty

Ear Infections

Because of that long, beautiful hair, Lhasa Apsos are prone to ear infections. The hair can get into the ear canals, giving bacteria a place to fester. The following are the common symptoms of an ear infection:

- Constant scratching of the ear
- Crusting or scabs in the ears
- Dark discharge
- Head shaking
- Odor near the ear
- Redness and swelling of the ear canal

If you notice these symptoms, get your dog to the vet. There are a number of topical treatments available, though your intelligent Lhasa Apso won't take long to learn what you plan to do and will attempt to prevent it. Most dogs hate having medicine put in their ears, so treatment will probably need to involve something that your dog loves as a follow-up to the torturous ways of treating an ear infection.

Eye Problems

Between their shorter noses and long hair, it is not a surprise that Lhasa Apsos are prone to a number of eye problems. Fortunately, none of these problems are fatal. Monitoring your Lhasa Apso can help you ensure that he doesn't suffer any serious eye problems.

CHERRY EYE

Glandular hypertrophy, better known as cherry eye, is caused by the third eyelid becoming inflamed. When this happens, you will be able to see the eyelid as it distends outward. Although it looks horrible, it is easily treated through surgery.

KERATITIS SICCA

Better known as dry eye, Lhasa Apsos tend to suffer from this because of the large size of their eyes and the way they protrude. The disease makes their tear glands less productive, so their eyes are not kept as moist as they should be. This can cause your dog to have itchy eyes, which can also encourage infections. If you notice your Lhasa Apso pawing at his face or rubbing it on different things around your house, take him to the vet. There are ointments that can help, but you need to discuss your options with your vet and get some help in learning how to treat your Lhasa Apso's eyes.

PROGRESSIVE RETINAL ATROPHY

PRA causes light sensitivity because of problems with the retina. Puppies should be tested, so if you adopt your puppy from a breeder, you should have a guarantee against this particular problem.

Dogs with this condition usually start presenting with night blindness, which can make your dog more nervous. If you look at your dog's eyes, they may also reflect light more as the eyes deteriorate. The ailment affects both eyes, so the problem should show in both. There is no treatment for the condition. You will need to learn to accommodate your dog's failing sight over time.

Photo Courtesy
of Natalie Bond

Lissencephaly

The most serious genetic problem with Lhasa Apsos, lissencephaly, is a very rare disorder where an animal's brain doesn't grow properly, and a part of it remains smaller than it should be and has fewer wrinkles than it ought to have.

The problem is usually fairly obvious during the first year, with the dog acting strangely. It may react aggressively to nothing, become confused without an obvious cause, or act depressed or hyperactive. It will walk without issue, but it will have problems when it runs, appearing to be very uncoordinated. Some affected dogs are blind, and others may have seizures.

Unfortunately, there is no cure for lissencephaly, and the only treatment is to help control the seizures. It is recommended that if a dog has lissencephaly, he should not be used to breed. If a dog is blind because of the disease, it is best to keep him in a place that is familiar so that he does not hurt himself.

You should talk to your vet if you suspect your dog has this condition. It is best to make sure he is carefully monitored, so you will need to keep in close contact with your vet to provide the most comfortable life possible for your dog.

Patellar Luxation / Luxating Patella

Luxating patella is a kneecap disease that is common in Lhasa Apsos. This ailment is genetic, and your dog's knee cap may be dislocated.

If your dog has this problem, you may notice that he is skipping a step or limping on one leg. In more severe cases, your dog may not use the affected leg, meaning he hops around on three legs. When the kneecap slips back into place, your dog will resume a normal walk. As a dog ages, this problem will become worse as other issues present themselves, such as hip or elbow dysplasia or arthritis, all of which can impair your dog's ability to walk.

For more severe cases, vets can perform surgery. Most dogs will not require surgery, but you need to make sure that your dog does not overeat or become overweight, as this will make walking that much harder.

Sebaceous Adenitis

This is a skin disease that destroys the sebaceous glands, which produce lubricating secretions and can cause scales and hair loss. It is not life-threatening—it is a cosmetic problem. Your dog probably won't even notice the problem unless he has another kind of skin infection too (which can be promoted by the disease).

It is a genetic disease, so your vet will need details regarding the parents' health. If that is not possible, your vet will run a few tests to determine if the condition is something to worry about.

If your pup has sebaceous adenitis, the vet will probably suggest a topical or oral therapy to help reduce the effects. This treatment might also include an antibiotic to treat any secondary infections.

Urinary Stones

Urinary stones can form in either the kidneys or bladder, and they are a more common problem for Lhasa Apsos than most other breeds. It makes them more prone to having accidents inside, and in more severe cases, it can cause blood in your dog's urine. Stones are uncomfortable to painful, and the best way to treat a dog with this potential problem is to prevent the stones from forming. The stones are a result of the accumulation of calcium oxalate, and they travel through the urinary system until they pass through and out of your dog (humans can also get stones). They are actually not fully understood, making it difficult to make recommendations without consulting a vet.

Your vet can conduct tests to check for potential issues, which usually present as high protein levels. This can be done as a part of the annual checkup, and if the vet detects a problem, it is likely that you will need to change your dog's diet. This will be done on an individual basis, so you will need to ensure that you follow your vet's recommendations until you find the right diet for your dog.

Common Owner Mistakes

> *Many pet owners are guilty of overfeeding. An overweight Lhasa is an unhealthy Lhasa. Too much weight will put a strain on their joints. Work with your vet to maintain a healthy body weight.*
>
> CHOO MICHAEL YANG
> *Yangchoo Lhasa Apso*

While every breed has its own set of genetic ailments, there are some health problems that are common to all dogs. These problems are largely a result of people not properly taking care of their dogs. There are things you can do that could unintentionally damage your dog's health; these mistakes are related to diet and exercise levels. In the puppy stage, it is a difficult balance to strike as your puppy is curious and enthusiastic. Even when he is a fully grown dog, you have to make sure you are minimizing how much stress is placed on your Lhasa Apso's body. Weight management is one important way of keeping your dog healthy. Since they can have problems with their back legs and back, you want to make sure there isn't too much strain on your dog due to overeating or a life that is too sedentary.

Prevention and Monitoring

As Chapter 18 covers, as dogs age, they start to slow down. However, it is important to keep an eye out for issues long before your dog reaches the senior years. Failing to notice early signs of potential issues can be detrimental or even fatal to your Lhasa Apso. Any changes in your Lhasa Apso's behavior are likely a sign of some-thing that should be checked by your vet. Symptoms like lethargy and loss of appetite are poten-tial signs of a lot of more serious issues, so if you notice your dog's behaviors or personality changing, it is best to take him to the vet.

Photo Courtesy of Caroline Major

Checking your Lhasa Apso's weight is important and should be done at least twice a year. You and your vet should keep an eye on your dog's weight, as being overweight puts a strain on your dog's back, legs, joints, and muscles. This can prevent a lot of health problems that are not breed-specific.

CHAPTER 18

The Aging Lhasa Apso

> *Your loving, loyal friend will slow down in his later years, want to sleep late in the morning, and take frequent naps during the day. But my dear 15 year old boy continues to follow me from room to room, lounging in a bed placed in each room just for him. He doesn't hear like he used to, so hand signals are used. Older ones require more patience and understanding and attention to health ailments that may develop. Short haircuts are preferred as the brushing and combing that they enjoyed as youngsters is no longer pleasurable. But they continue to enjoy snuggling and their regular routine, even occasionally a game with a favorite toy.*
>
> KATHLEEN WALCOTT
> *Floral Hill Lhasa Apsos*

On average, Lhasa Apsos live between 12 and 14 years, but it isn't uncommon for the breed to live a good bit beyond that. Some have even managed to live over 20 years. This means that you will probably have a pretty good length of time with your adorable Lhasa Apso. But no matter how old your dog is, it is never going to feel like you had enough time together.

Lhasa Apsos are considered seniors by the time they are 10 years old. You will probably notice your dog slowing down around eight or nine years old, and by 10, you will notice that your Lhasa Apso doesn't have quite as much energy and will probably walk a little more stiffly than in previous years. A dog may remain healthy his whole life, but as the years start to take their toll, his body may not be able to enjoy the same activities.

Photo Courtesy
of Jane Wenckus

The first signs of aging usually appear as stiffness in the gait or heavy panting that begins early in your walk. If you see these changes, start to cut back on the long walks and go for shorter ones more often. Your Lhasa Apso may want to continue to be active, which calls for an adjustment in his activities but not a complete stop.

Be sure your pup doesn't overexert himself if he tries to remain active. Your Lhasa Apso may not want to accept the fact that things are changing. Fortunately for your Lhasa Apso, he will usually remain fairly happy as long as he is able to just lounge with you—it's one of the major benefits of having such an affable dog. He is always happy just being with his family, so he isn't going to be nearly so upset about losing his ability to be as active as many other breeds.

Another early symptom of aging in Lhasa Apsos is vision and hearing loss. The haze in your dog's eyes is a sign that his vision isn't quite what it used to be and could be a sign of cataracts. If you notice your dog being less aware of his surroundings, talk about this with your vet. Lhasa Apsos usually don't go completely blind or deaf, but you will want to know if his ability to see or hear is impaired.

There is a reason this period of time is called the golden years—you can relax and enjoy this time of your dog's life as well. You don't have to worry about him tearing up things because he's bored or becoming overexcited when seeing a squirrel during his walks. Instead, you can enjoy lazy evenings, peaceful weekends, and less strenuous exercise. It's easy to make the senior years incredibly enjoyable for your Lhasa Apso and yourself by making the necessary adjustments.

Senior Care Challenges – Common Physical Disorders Related to Aging

Accommodations you should make for your senior Lhasa Apso include:

- Set water bowls in a couple of different places so that your dog can reach them easily.
- Cover hard floor surfaces (such as tile, hardwood, and vinyl) with nonslip carpets or rugs.
- Use cushions and softer bedding for your Lhasa Apso to make things more comfortable. There are even bed warmers for dogs if your Lhasa Apso displays achy joints or muscles. You also need to make sure he isn't too warm, so this can be a fine balancing act.
- To improve his circulation, increase how often you brush your Lhasa Apso.
- Keep your dog inside in extreme heat or cold. An old canine cannot handle changes in temperature as well as he once did.
- Use stairs or ramps so that your old pup doesn't have to do any jumping.
- Avoid moving furniture around in your home, particularly if your Lhasa Apso shows signs of problems with his eyesight or if he has dementia. A familiar home is more comforting and less stressful for your pet as he ages. If your Lhasa Apso isn't able to see as clearly as he once did, you should make sure his surroundings remain familiar to him, which will make it easier for him to move around without hurting himself.
- Consider setting up an area for your dog that allows him to avoid stairs, especially if climbing seems to bother him.
- Create a space with fewer distractions and noises where your Lhasa Apso can relax. Don't make your old friend feel isolated; instead, give him a place where he can get away from everyone if he needs to be alone.
- Be prepared to let your dog go outside for restroom breaks more often.

Previous chapters address illnesses that are common in a Lhasa Apso. However, old age tends to bring a slew of ailments that are not particular to any one breed. Here are other things you will need to watch for (as well as talking to your vet about if they occur):

DID YOU KNOW?
Pet Loss
Support Groups

Losing a pet can feel like losing a beloved family member, but you don't need to grieve alone. Pet loss support groups can be found in almost any community and are a great way to process your feelings of grief among peers who understand what you're going through. Contact your local Humane Society or veterinarian to see what grief support services are available in your area.

- Arthritis is probably the most common ailment in any dog breed, and the Lhasa Apso is no exception. If your dog is experiencing stiffness and pain after normal activities, talk with your vet about ways to help minimize your Lhasa Apso's discomfort.

- Gum disease is a common issue in older dogs as well, and you should continue brushing your dog's teeth on a regular basis as he ages. A regular check of your Lhasa Apso's teeth and gums can help ensure no problem develops.

- Loss of eyesight or blindness is relatively common in older dogs, just as it is in humans. Have your dog's vision checked at least once a year or more often if it is obvious his eyesight is failing.

- Kidney disease is a frequent problem in older dogs and one that you should watch for as your Lhasa Apso ages. If your canine drinks a lot of water and has accidents frequently, take him to the vet as soon as possible.

- Although diabetes is usually thought of as a genetic condition, any Lhasa Apso can become diabetic if not fed and exercised properly.

Vet Visits – The Importance of Regular Vet Visits and What to Expect

As your Lhasa Apso ages, slowing down and occasional pain will become obvious. If your Lhasa Apso has a debilitating ailment or condition, discuss options for giving him a better quality of life. For example, wheelchairs are available if your Lhasa Apso shows problems with mobility.

Just as humans visit the doctor more often as they age, you'll need to take your dog to see your vet with greater frequency, too. The vet can make sure your Lhasa Apso stays active without overdoing it, and he can help alleviate unnecessary stress in your dog's life.

Based on your Lhasa Apso's changing personality and physical abilities, your vet might recommend changes to your dog's daily schedule and

Photo Courtesy of Nicole James

to his typical activities to keep your Lhasa Apso happy and active during the later years.

The following are the kinds of things to expect when you go to the vet:

- Your vet will talk about your dog's history even if you have visited every year. This conversation is necessary to see how your dog's life has changed over time and to pinpoint when problems manifested themselves or got worse.

- Your vet will probably conduct a complete physical examination to assess your dog's current health.

- Depending on your dog's age and on his health, your vet may want to run some tests. The following are some of the most common tests for older dogs:

  - Arthropod-borne disease testing, which involves drawing blood and testing it for viral infections
  - Chemistry screening for kidney, liver, and sugar evaluation
  - Complete blood count
  - Fecal flotation, which involves mixing your dog's poop with a special liquid to test for worms and other parasites
  - Heartworm testing
  - Urinalysis, which tests your dog's urine to check the health of his kidneys and urinary system
  - Routine wellness check, which the vet has been conducting on your dog for years
  - Any breed-specific tests for your aging Lhasa Apso

Changes That Might Occur

Keep an eye out for different signs that your dog is slowing down. This will help you to know when to adjust the setup around your home and to reduce how much your old pup is exercising.

Appetite and Nutritional Requirements

With less exercise, your dog won't need as many calories as usual, which means you will need to adjust his diet. If you opted to feed your Lhasa Apso commercial dog food, make sure to switch to a senior dog formula. Senior

Photo Courtesy of Wendy Rosen

food is designed for the changing dietary needs of older dogs by including fewer calories and adding more nutrients.

If you prepare dog food at home, talk to your vet and research how best to reduce calories without sacrificing taste. Your canine is going to need less fat in his diet, so you should make healthier food choices while still considering the taste. These dietary changes will be different from the puppy and active adult foods you fed your Lhasa Apso in the past.

Exercise

It's up to you to adjust your dog's schedule and to keep him less active yet happy. Shorter and more frequent walks should take care of your Lhasa Apso's exercise needs, as well as helping to break up your day a little more.

Your dog will enjoy napping as much as walking, especially if he gets to cuddle with you. Sleeping beside you while you watch television or as you nap is pretty much all it takes to make your older Lhasa Apso content!

You may notice your Lhasa Apso spends more time sniffing during walks, which could be a sign that your dog is tiring. If he is walking slower, looking up at you, and flopping down, that could be his way of letting you know it's time to return home. If your canine can no longer manage long walks, make them shorter and more often. You could also spend more time romping around your yard or at home with your buddy.

Aging and the Senses

Just like people, dogs' senses weaken as they get older. They won't hear things as well as they used to, they won't see things as clearly, and their sense of smell will weaken.

The following are some of the signs your dog is losing at least one of his senses:

- It becomes easy to surprise or startle your dog. You need to be careful because this can make your Lhasa Apso aggressive.

- Your dog may seem to ignore you or is less responsive when you issue a command.

- Cloudy eyes may be a sign of sight loss, though it does not mean your dog is blind.

If your aging dog seems to "behave badly," it is a sign that he is aging, not that he wants to rebel. Do not punish your older dog.

Adjust your schedule to meet your dog's changing abilities. Adjust his water bowl's height, refrain from rearranging rooms, and pet your dog more often. Make sure his bed is fluffy, or get him a new, more comfortable bed. Put the bed on the floor if it was previously kept on furniture. Your dog is probably nervous about losing his abilities, so it is up to you to comfort him.

Keeping Your Senior Dog Mentally Active

Just because your older Lhasa Apso can't walk as far as he used to doesn't mean his brain is weaker too. As long as your Lhasa Apso performs all of the basic commands, you can teach him all kinds of new, low-impact tricks.

At this point, training could be easier because your Lhasa Apso has learned to focus better, and he'll be happy to have something he can still do with you. New toys are another fun way to help keep your dog's mind active. Be careful the toys aren't too rough on your dog's jaw and teeth. There are also food balls, puzzles, and other games that focus on cognitive abilities—and games such as hide and seek will still be very much appreciated!

Some senior dogs suffer from cognitive dysfunction syndrome (CCD), a type of dementia. It is estimated that 85 percent of all cases of dementia in dogs go undiagnosed because of the difficulty in pinpointing the problem. It manifests itself more as a problem of temperament than of cognitive ability.

If your dog begins to act differently, you should take him to the vet to see if he has CCD. While there really isn't any treatment for this problem, your vet can recommend things that will help your dog focus. An action such as rearranging the furniture is strongly discouraged because your dog relies on the familiarity of his surroundings to reduce his stress.

Mental stimulation at this time of your Lhasa Apso's life is also still a must. Not only will keeping his mind active fight CCD, but it will also keep him healthy whether he exhibits signs of dementia or not.

Advantages to the Senior Years

The last years of your Lhasa Apso's life can be just as enjoyable (if not more so) than the earlier stages since your dog has mellowed over time. All those high-energy activities will give way to relaxing and enjoying time with you. Your Lhasa Apso will continue to be a loving companion, interacting with you at every opportunity. That does not change with age. However, your canine's limitations should dictate interactions and activities. If you are busy, make sure you schedule time with your Lhasa Apso to do things that are within those limitations. It is just as easy to make an older Lhasa Apso happy as it is to make a young dog happy!

Preparing to Say Goodbye

No pet parent wants to think about this last step, but as you watch your Lhasa Apso slow down, you will know when your time with your sweet pup is coming to an end. Some dogs can continue to live for years after they begin to slow down, but many dogs don't make it more than a year or two. Sometimes dogs will lose their interest in eating, will have a stroke, or another problem will arise without warning. Eventually, it will be time to say goodbye, whether at home or at the vet's office. You need to be prepared.

Talk to your family about how you should care for your dog over the last few years or months of his life. Many dogs will be perfectly happy, continuing life as usual, despite their limited abilities. Some may begin to have problems controlling their bowel movements, while others may have problems getting up from a prone position. There are solutions to all of these problems. Always remember that quality of life should be your primary concern. Since your dog cannot tell you how he feels, you must take cues from your Lhasa Apso. If your dog still seems happy, there is no reason to have him euthanized.

At this stage, your dog is probably happy just sleeping near you for eighteen hours a day. This is perfectly fine as long as he still gets excited about walking, eating, and being petted. The purpose of euthanasia is to reduce suffering, not to make things more convenient for yourself. This is what makes the decision so difficult, but your dog's behavior should be a fairly good indicator of how he is feeling. Here are some other things to watch when evaluating your dog's quality of life:

- Appetite
- Drinking
- Urinating and defecation
- Pain (noted by excessive panting)
- Stress levels
- Desire to be active or with family (If your dog wants to be alone most of the time, this is usually a sign he is trying to be alone for the end of his life.)

Photo Courtesy of Tori Piper

Talk to your vet if your dog has a serious illness to determine the best path forward. They can provide the best information on the quality of your dog's life and how long your dog is likely to live with his disease or ailment.

If your dog gets to the point where he is no longer happy, he can't move around, or he has a fatal illness, it is probably time to say goodbye. This is a decision that should be made as a family, always putting the dog's needs and quality of life first. If you decide it is time to say goodbye, determine who will be present at the end.

If you have decided to euthanize your dog, you can make his last few minutes calming and peaceful by feeding your dog the things he couldn't eat before. Foods like chocolate and grapes can put a smile on his face for his remaining time in your life.

You can also have your dog euthanized at home. If you decide to request a vet to come to your home, be prepared for additional charges for the home visit. You also need to determine where you want your dog to be, whether inside or outside, and in which room if you decide to do it inside.

Make sure at least one person he knows well is present so that your dog is not alone during the last few minutes of his life. You don't want your dog to die surrounded by strangers. The process is fairly peaceful, but your dog will probably be a little stressed. He will pass within a few minutes of the injection but continue to talk to him, as his brain will continue to work even after his eyes close.

Once your dog is gone, you need to determine what to do with the body:

- **Cremation** is one of the most common ways of taking care of the body. You can request an urn or ask for a container for his ashes so you can scatter your dog's ashes over his favorite places. Make sure you don't spread his ashes in places where this action is not permitted. Private cremation is more expensive than communal cremation, but it means the only ashes you receive are from your dog. Communal cremation occurs when several pets are cremated together.

- **Burial** is the easiest method after your dog is euthanized and can be performed at your home. However, you need to check local regulations to be sure burying your dog on your property is legal. You also need to consider the soil; if your yard is rocky or sandy, that will create problems when trying to bury your pet. Also, don't bury your pet in a spot that is near a well that people use as a drinking source or if it is near wetlands or waterways. Your dog's body can contaminate the water as it decays. You can also look into a pet cemetery if there is one in your area.

Grief and Healing

Dogs become members of our families, so their passing can be incredibly difficult. People go through all of the same emotions and feelings of loss with a dog as they do with close friends and family. The absence of your dog's presence in your life is jarring, especially with such a loving, loyal dog like the Lhasa Apso. It will feel weird not to have that presence by your side as you move around your home, and it will be a constant reminder of your loss. In the beginning, you and your family will probably feel considerable grief. Saying goodbye will be extremely difficult, so taking a couple of days off work is not a bad idea. While some people might say your Lhasa Apso was "just a dog," you know better; it is okay to feel the pain and to grieve as you would for any lost loved one.

Losing your Lhasa Apso is also going to create a substantial change in your schedule. It will probably take a while to become accustomed to the shift in your day-to-day life. Fight the urge to go out and get a new dog because you almost certainly will not be ready yet.

Everyone grieves differently, so allow yourself to grieve in a way that is healthy for you. Everyone in your family will feel the loss differently, too, so let them do the same. Some people don't require much time, while others can feel the loss for months. There is no timetable, so don't try to force it on yourself or on any member of your family.

Talk about how you would like to remember your pup. You can have a memorial for your lost pet, tell stories, or plant a tree in your dog's memory.

Try to return to your normal routine as much as possible if you have other pets. This can be both painful and helpful as your other pets will still need you just as much as when your Lhasa Apso was alive. This is especially true of your other dogs, who have also lost their companion.

If you find grief is hindering your ability to function normally, seek professional help. If needed, you can search online to find support groups in your area to help you and your family, especially if this was your first dog. Sometimes it helps to talk about the loss so that you can begin to heal.

Printed in the USA
CPSIA information can be obtained
at www.ICGtesting.com
LVHW072138101123
763491LV00011B/965